BRAVER THAN THE NIGHT

Richard Picardi

SCHOLASTIC INC.
New York Toronto London Auckland Sydney Tokyo

ISBN 0-590-32879-4

Copyright © 1983 by Richard Picardi. All rights reserved. Published by Scholastic Inc.

12 11 10 9 8 7 6 5 4 3 2 1   9   3 4 5 6 7/8

To Judy and Betsy,
to Dennis and Kevin —

they still believe in dreams.

ONE

Even as Owen lay dying, a memory still lived inside him of a time when he was happy. It was a time when they were all together — his father and mother, his older brother Chris, and the younger ones, Peter and Suzanne. That was before his father left them and went away somewhere. That was before he made a phone call and found out Chris was dead.

Back then even school wasn't bad at all. Owen only had to walk a few blocks to get there, and on the first day the principal even leaned over to him and said, "So you're Chris Thomas's brother!" He smiled when the other kids looked over, and he shouted "Yup!" so loudly that he startled even Sr. Edna, the nun the kids called "the Warden."

And when he went to bed at night, his brothers beside him, he could hear his parents' voices, dreamy together, in the next room. So for a time he felt warm and safe and protected. But then he started waking up in the dark, frightened by his parents' shouting.

"Don't ask me where I went, I went out. I'll go out whenever the hell I want to!"

"Shh, Bobby, please. You'll wake the children."

Then it would grow quiet again, enough for him to hear his brothers move in the dark. And in the mornings he thought that the noises in the night might only have been nightmares.

But one night when he was eight years old, his eyes blinked open.

"I saw you with her. I saw you!"

"You're crazy, Judy. You didn't see nothing."

Suddenly Owen gasped, and his hand jerked up to protect himself from the ghost-like face above him. A quick hand grabbed his, and he realized it was Chris, awakened by the shouting. He was sitting on the edge of his bed, his already big shoulders hunched over, his face pale and whitened in the dim light from the street lamp outside their window. They sat huddled together in the dark, listening to their parents' quarrels.

"What the hell! Are you spying on me?"

"I wasn't spying. I saw you coming out of her house when I took my mother to the doctor's. If you don't care about me, at least don't carry on where the children can see you."

"The children, the children. That's all I ever hear around here."

"Shh. Now Suzanne's crying."

"Let her cry. I don't care if the whole damn world cries. If it wasn't for you and those damn kids I'd be out there quarterbacking with the Jets instead of working in the stinking fish markets."

Owen turned over on his side and began to cry softly as the front door slammed shut. He felt a hand gently rub his shoulder.

"C'mon, O. No tears. Daddy says it's weak to cry."

Chris opened the door and went to his mother, who was trying to quiet Suzanne. Six-year-old Peter slept through it all. Despite his brother's encouraging words, Owen cried until he fell asleep.

It was very quiet when Owen woke up. He thought maybe it was Saturday and they didn't have to get up for school. He went down into the kitchen and saw Chris sitting at the table, speaking quietly with his mother.

"Where's Daddy?"

"Shut up, O. Get ready for school!" yelled Chris. Owen ducked as an empty Cheerios box whizzed over his head.

It was three months before they saw their father again.

* * *

In June Mrs. Thomas received a call from school. They didn't have to tell her it was about Owen. She felt almost resigned as she walked into Sr. Edna's office.

"Good morning, Mrs. Thomas."

"Good morning, Sister. Sorry I'm late. I couldn't get someone to mind the baby. How are my boys doing?"

"Oh, they're wonderful boys, really. Full of jokes Christopher is. And Peter has started out very well."

Mrs. Thomas couldn't help it, but she started wondering where Sr. Edna kept the gallons of Windex she must have used to keep the glass on her desk shining. There wasn't a single spot or book on it. She knew the axe was about to fall. "And Owen?"

"He's having serious problems, Mrs. Thomas — very serious. In the past few months he seems to have forgotten everything. It's as if he never learned how to read or do the most basic arithmetic. I'd like you and his father to agree to have Owen repeat the third grade."

Mrs. Thomas was so stunned she didn't speak.

"You don't have to decide right now. Talk it over with your husband first."

"No, that won't be necessary. If you think this is best for Owen now, it's okay."

"Are you sure you don't want time to discuss it with your husband?"

"Sister Edna, I don't even know where my husband is!"

The retort was so sharp and unexpected that the nun felt as if she'd been slapped. But in that second when their eyes met, she saw that Owen's mother, so young and pretty, had tears in her eyes. Her sisterly heart was filled with useless compassion.

Eventually even the neighborhood kids caught on that the Thomas kids' father wasn't around anymore. And naturally any good city kid worth his territory was quick to spot a weak point. One day Billy Mascarella started the taunts from a block away.

"Hey, Owen, where's your father? On the moon?"

And Chris yelled back, "Hang it up, Mascarella. At least I know who my father is, Mashface!"

But when Danny Cassaza started in with his made-up, adolescent leer about Chris's mother and father not "getting it on," Owen just charged up the block and punched him right in the nose. Peter let out a yell and they all crashed together, clawing and punching and shouting the newest swear words they had picked up. But it was no contest. Billy and Danny ran away as soon as they scrambled free. And Owen and Peter, with energy to spare, ganged up on their big brother Chris, who answered with shouts and mock pleas for mercy. And soon all three were rolling around on the ground, laughing about how they made the stupid idiots run away.

That summer they left their home and moved in with Mrs. Thomas's father. He had plenty of room and was lonely now with his wife dead and his son Tom in Vietnam. Christopher once heard his grandfather complain about having cramps, and from then on "Gramps" was his name. Gramps lived nearby, so the boys stayed in the same grammar school as before, with Owen now unhappily three years behind Chris instead of two, and Peter one year behind Owen.

Mrs. Thomas, a nurse, began to work nights at the hospital so that she could see her children off in the morning and be there when they came home in the afternoon. It didn't leave her much time to sleep — an hour or two here and there, if she was lucky — but being with her growing children helped her survive and even remain cheerful through it all.

When the fall came the boys were all together for football, playing for the Hurricanes just as they had when their father enrolled them. How they used to love cutting straight across the field beside him! Only Danny Collins's father was almost as big, but even he hadn't tried out for the Jets like their father! Christopher was the quarterback, punter, and kicker all in one. Owen was the halfback, and Peter played the line. At the end of the season Owen and Peter stayed in the Peewee division, while Chris got his new uniform and moved up to the Ponies.

After football season there was swimming and track. Owen liked running the most, not just because it came naturally to him, but because he always won. And as long as he won he didn't have to worry about facing his father's anger, the way he used to after a swimming meet. His father wanted him to play sports, but most of all he wanted his son to be tough — and to win.

Then there were the local basketball teams and the Saturday morning leagues at St. Vinnie's. Peter didn't make the team because he had gotten heavy and didn't have the speed, but Owen made it easily, and Chris became the star. His mother noticed that Chris had begun to practice his shots everyday all by himself at the hoop that crowned Gramps's garage. One late afternoon, while getting ready to work the night shift at the hospital, she realized the sound had changed. It was a hard, snapping rhythm, not the unsteady bouncing of a child. She went to the window expecting to see a stranger in the backyard below. Instead, she saw Chris leaping up to reach the rim with his fingertips in the sold-out Madison Square Garden of his imagination. How could she have missed it! It must have happened one night when she was on duty. Her son had gone through the fearsome and wonderful change into manhood. He was still fair, his hair was still a golden brown, his eyes blue, but suddenly he was taut and angled instead of soft and rounded as when he had slept in her lap.

"Bravo, Chris!" she yelled down to her handsome son. He looked up to his mother with a smile so bright that she felt a lump of joy swell in her throat.

TWO

The following April, Chris, Owen, and Peter were out in the parade grounds for the track meets. Peter was sitting out the quarter-mile, but Owen and Chris were running hard and close. Owen suddenly realized he was alone, ahead of the pack. As he glanced back he saw his brother falling off by the side of the track. Then he heard a voice yelling: "Chris, what'd you do, have a heart attack? Get in there. Get tough."

It was their father.

He took them out to dinner that night and bought presents for them as well. After he dropped them off at home in Brooklyn he went back to the city or somewhere in the Hamptons. They weren't sure. They didn't see him again for two years.

On another April morning, two years later, Chris packed his gym bag and basketball and

raced out of the new home that his mother
and his Uncle Tom had bought. It was a nice
house with three bedrooms upstairs and one
more in the attic that Chris claimed for his
own. When he had really made it his own, it
would be called "the Pit."

Waving good-bye to his mother, Chris took
the four outside steps in one leap and headed
for the subway. He was on his way to the
Annual Police Basketball Shoot-out. He knew
there would be kids from all over New York
competing there, and he was ready to take
them all on — not just for the prize of a week
in Willis Reed's basketball camp, but for the
sheer fun of it. Chris loved basketball, no
doubt about it.

Once inside the cavernous armory, Chris
glanced around for a familiar face until he
spotted a kid wearing a jacket from St.
Thomas's, a school near his own in Brooklyn.

"How ya doin'! I'm Chris Thomas from St.
Vinnie's. What's your name?"

"Hi, I'm Boyle. Kevin Boyle."

"You have a brother Brian?"

"Yeah, I do. You know him?"

"Sure, I saw him play for Nazareth last
winter. Good hands. Great jumper. Your
mom's in Parents Without Partners, like
mine, right?"

Kevin just nodded his head. He was by
nature shy and pensive, and he had never
met anyone quite like this Thomas charac-

ter, standing over six feet tall and smiling from ear to ear.

"Your parents divorced, too?" Chris asked, pulling off his jacket.

"No. My father died. Two years ago."

"Well, Boyle, I guess we're sort of in the same boat — Partners Without Pops. Now let's play some basketball and show these dudes how it's done!"

At the end of the day Kevin still couldn't figure Chris out. Here was someone who could talk about Parents Without Partners and go right on smiling. Kevin kept his father's death close to him like a secret no one must know. As if he had complicity in it. As if by hiding the injury it would hurt less. This Thomas character, though, talked freely about such things and somehow made Kevin feel better, more confident. What Kevin didn't understand then was that just because Chris smiled and encouraged him didn't mean that he didn't have his own deep need for reassuring companionship. Nor could Kevin have guessed back then that this laughing kid he had just met might have hurts of his own that he kept hidden deep inside.

But whatever else he thought at the time, Kevin was beginning to think he had found a new friend. And by the final round of the shoot-out on May nineteenth, Kevin was sure of two things: He did have a new friend and Chris was one good basketball player. Actually Chris and Kevin were both good, and after graduation from grammar school were on their way to Willis Reed's.

Willis, a superstar in the glory day of the New York Knicks, had located his basketball camp on the majestic banks of the Hudson River. Chris arrived there in July and from a hilltop took in the sight of the trees, the huge sky, and the river curving in the distance below. He had never seen anything like this before: so calm and quiet and beautiful.

"Thom–ass!" The joyful, innocent vulgarity echoed in the valley. It was Kevin. Chris charged down the hill, and the two raced to the dorms to find their room. When they found it, there was a big kid named Dennis Greaney standing in the hall outside his room.

"Chris, this is Dennis Greaney from St. Thomas."

"Hiya doin', Greeny."

"It's pronounced Grainy."

"Okay, Grainy. Don't go grievin' on me!"

Dennis pushed his door open and went in, followed by Kevin and by Chris, who immediately started to pantomime dribbling and shooting. As Dennis went to open the window, Chris scooped up a jock that was on a chair and executed a lightning pass.

"Heads up, Greeny!"

Dennis glanced over his shoulder just in time to see his jock sail out the window and down to the ledge below.

"You crazy airhead, go get it!"

Chris shrugged, "Okay, Greeny," and raced downstairs. The door he knocked on was opened by the biggest, blackest coach he had ever seen. Without hesitating Chris said, "Excuse me. Mind if I get that jock off your windowsill?" Then he grabbed a plate off a hallway table and ran upstairs.

When Dennis opened his door there was Chris — a broad smile shining in his face, a towel draped over his arm, and at shoulder-level a plate with Dennis's jock on top of it.

"Jock *du jour,* Greeny?"

THREE

In September, when Chris and Kevin walked up to the front entrance, Nazareth High School was still shrouded in scaffolding from the fire that had ravaged it in February. Rumor had it that the mob had it torched because the school let the police and the FBI use it for surveillance of the drug trafficking headquartered in a trailer in the auto junkyard behind the school. But others said the mob would never start a fire in a chapel. Anyway, everyone had gotten out safely, and the reconstruction was beginning when Chris and Kevin started their freshman year.

Both were put in the top classes because of their high aptitude scores. In October they went through the basketball tryouts and became starters on the freshman team. If Kevin had found a new friend since the

Police Shoot-out, Chris had left his brother Owen behind and had just about found a new brother in Kevin.

In December of that year almost all of the students in the all-boys school, and many of the teachers, were wearing the long hair of the Woodstock generation. Chris and Kevin went out and got crew cuts.

Mr. Perillo, the chairman of the English Department, was at his office desk one day when a laughing, quizzical-eyed kid stuck his head in the door. It was Kevin. Suddenly another head veered into the doorway over his. Actually, it struck Mr. Perillo more like ten-percent head — the other ninety-percent was a huge grin.

"Nice head, Kevin. Who's your friend?"

"This is Chris Thomas."

Mr. Settanni, who taught freshman English, turned from his desk to take in the scene.

"Hiya doin, Mr. S.!" Chris called over. "Mark our papers yet?"

Before he could answer, there was an unseen elbow jab, a burst of laughter, and down the hallway the two boys disappeared with Chris shouting, "C'mon, Baldy, we'll be late for practice!"

Mr. Settanni walked over to his chairman. "You mean you haven't met the "Baldwin Brothers" yet?"

"No, only Kevin. What a pair of characters."

"I'm not sure Naz High is ready for those two. They can both write, though, especially Boyle."

So only a week later Dan Perillo had them both working on freshman basketball for the yearbook. When the book came out it recorded Chris's 25 points, 17 rebounds against Nazareth's rival, Xaverian High School. Kevin, after a disappointing winter of sitting out most games, proved at last to his coach what he could do by scoring seventeen points against a big suburban team and sixteen against a tough league rival. Chris was named Most Valuable Player for the season. The yearbook headline read, "Frosh's 7–3 Almost Championship Season. We may be Number One."

In the fall a long teachers' strike delayed the opening of the school year for nearly six weeks. After hearing increasing rumors that their school might shut down altogether, Chris and Kevin were both glad when it did reopen and basketball tryouts were scheduled. Although Kevin had to settle for the junior varsity team, Chris was elated to move directly up to varsity, especially since he would be playing with Dennis Kelly, a junior. Chris had played basketball with Dennis throughout grammar school and had always admired the seriousness and dedication that he showed, although he wasn't yet ready to be quite so serious himself.

At his debut varsity practice under the

team's new coach Pete Gillen, with almost every player in the school's maroon gym shorts and gray shirts, Chris came running on the court in the wildest green-and-yellow striped shorts, shirt, kneepads, and headband that anyone had ever seen. His new teammates loved it. Coach Gillen promptly sent him to the showers. Dennis laughed so hard that he was sent to join him.

A week later when Mr. Perillo was leaving school, Chris ran up and asked him for a ride.

"Sure, Chris. Going home early today? No practice?"

"Uh, no, I got excused."

As they drove along Perillo glanced over at his solemn passenger, wondering what had happened in just a few days to banish the joy of making varsity.

"Are you okay, Chris? Where's the old smile?"

"I'm okay, Mr. Perillo. Can you let me off here? I have to get the subway and go and see my father."

"Oh, sure. Your father? Is he back home?"

Chris looked quickly at Perillo as he opened the car door — a look at once sad and puzzled, as if he wondered how a teacher, now a dean, could be so dense as to think his parents would be together.

At a game that winter with their greatest rival, Xaverian High School, Chris threw the only punch at another player that either

Dennis or Kevin could ever remember. Even when his friend Sully hit him in a pickup game a month before, Chris didn't hit him back, although he did get him with a cream pie a week later in the cafeteria.

It was also the only game that Chris's father ever attended, except for the one in which his son's number was retired, three weeks after he was killed.

If Kevin often seemed like Chris's twin and equal brother, then Dennis Kelly was soon to become the steady older brother that Chris didn't have — but surely needed. But not before Coach Gillen had gone to the dean's office several times and had resolved with Mr. Perillo that Dennis, who had lost his father and had been getting into trouble with a crowd neither one thought much of, would not surrender his bright promise without a fight. In the end, in solitude, Dennis stared in the eye of his own wasted future and decided that he was indeed worth fighting for. He became the varsity team's captain for the upcoming year and never turned back.

Chris, meanwhile, had started a little teenage rebellion of his own by junior year. In the Great Bavarian Beer Caper, he thought his mother had gone upstairs to nap before going to work. So he began passing cans of beer out the window to his co-conspirator Kevin, who had his gym bag hoisted above his head to receive the booty they planned to enjoy in the park that night after the game.

Kevin was so shocked when Chris's mother came up the driveway that he dropped the bag just as Chris flipped another can out the window. The can crashed on the cement and sent a geyser of beer spraying all over Mrs. Thomas. Chris was muttering, "Baldy, you jerk, you'll wake her up," as he stuck his head out the window. It didn't take him long to figure out he was in big trouble.

Trouble in Chris's house meant being grounded, that is, not allowed out of the house except for school for a set period of time.

"And don't you dare leave this house, young man. Your father will hear about this."

"Oh, Mom."

"Don't 'oh, Mom' me!"

"You know he doesn't give a damn about me. He never even comes to basketball games anymore to see me play. I'm not afraid of him anyway."

"We'll see about that! Now go upstairs, and if you walk out that door tonight, you'll be very sorry."

When his mother finally did take her overdue nap, with Chris's uniform under her pillow, he climbed out his bedroom window to the roof of the porch and then jumped to the backyard below. After Chris ran all the way to school for the game, the new coach Bill Burke benched him for the first quarter for "forgetting" his uniform. Otherwise Chris came away from the caper unscathed as usual.

That fall Chris paid little mind to his teachers' lectures about junior year being so important for college. He saw no more reason to worry about college than to worry about basketball or girls. A disappointing 2–12 season was in the past, and every lovely girl had suddenly found Chris Thomas all but irresistible. Every girl to him was Mt. Everest, and to his other talents Chris had recently added mountain climbing.

Dolores Kilgannon was five feet four inches and barely one hundred pounds when Chris spotted her in the crowded lobby after a game that December. Actually, he saw her bright red hair first, then her pretty face and white skin. Dee, as Chris soon called her, was so fair she got freckles when she walked past a sunlamp. She had also the most gentle of natures, like Chris's own in those days. No matter how many girls he would meet, or how many women would be attracted to him in the next four years, Chris would never love a single one of them the way he loved Dee.

All in all, except for her red hair, Dee was very much like Chris's mother, and she soon responded in the same way to whatever he did. Perhaps it was his joyous freedom as well as his good looks that delighted Dee. Her own upbringing was so closed and confining that Chris seemed to open a completely new and wonderful world for her. Chris was allowed almost anything and forgiven everything.

And why not? Who could imagine him doing anything really mean or malicious, and even if someone thought so, didn't that glorious smile make it go away? If he made a sarcastic remark about someone else's girl friend it was only meant as a joke — no need for a friend to get upset over it. The fact that such a remark wasn't quite the same as a cream pie thrown in the cafeteria that made everyone including teachers laugh, or that his own good looks might have made the stinging remark even more wounding, had yet to dawn on Chris Thomas. Perhaps love had come too easily for him to know its price.

FOUR

The varsity team did in fact have a surprising turnaround that year. Their previous losing season became a 15–7 won-loss record in Chris's junior year, but more importantly, they were building the best defensive unit in New York. And this would be essential if they were ever to achieve that distant dream of a City Championship. Dennis, renamed Den-Doo by Chris because he said his friend was a "can-do" man, would not be around to enjoy it. He was on his way to Siena College in upstate New York to pursue his basketball dream. But Kevin, who had moved up to varsity after winning the Most Valuable Player trophy on the junior varsity team, would be there, along with Kevin Dunleavy, Tom Dean, and Gerry O'Shea. Together they would help shape the formless dream that beckoned them.

In the spring, Chris took Dee to the Junior

Prom. The circle of friends — Elmo, Jug-head, Lubes, Ackie, T.H. Sully, Shrimp, and Kevin (he was Baldy only to Chris) — posed for a picture.

Soon they would drift off into the long summer afternoon before senior year.

Chris's brother Owen, meanwhile, had graduated from grammar school. After los-ing a year at the time of his parents' separa-tion, he had gradually regained his academic standing and applied to Nazareth, where Chris would soon be a senior. When he was only put on the waiting list and not certain of being admitted, Owen turned to La Salle Academy, but it was already too late, so he enrolled in public school at Midwood High. Unable to concentrate on his schoolwork, unable to make friends as quickly as his brother Chris, Owen soon grew restless and unhappy there.

When Chris returned to school that fall he was a little unhappy, too — it just wasn't the same without Dennis. Everything else was fine. He and Kevin were both in advanced placement classes for college credit. He had grown even taller and was now a six-foot-four-inch center. His game had improved, he was named the co-captain with Tom Dean, and the varsity tallied up an amazing seven straight victories before Christmas.

But he missed his friend. So in Novem-ber Chris made the five-hour bus journey to

Siena to see Dennis. In half an hour they were on the court. Chris, Dennis, his roommate Mark — a huge two hundred-and-sixty pounder, out of a southern military academy (Chris called him "the house") — and Alberto King, who had just gotten out of jail for robbing a supermarket. Al should have stuck to basketball. He committed the robbery wearing his Adelphi University basketball jacket with his name and numbers across the back, big as life. Chris took a liking to Alberto, and after a break Dennis and Mark resumed their game while Chris sat on the bench talking with Alberto for a hour and a half. It was undoubtedly the oddest foursome on any Division I court that year. Chris loved it, and Siena loved Chris.

That Chris can relate to anyone, Dennis thought to himself. *He can charm the blackest, he can charm the whitest.*

The only think Den-Doo worried about was Melanie, a beauty he had started to date. Dennis, somewhat unsure of himself with women, was well aware of Chris's ability to attract the prettiest of them like a magnet. Perhaps they were drawn by the tall, broad-shouldered size he got from his father, perhaps by the baby-faced handsomeness he got from his mother. Or maybe it was his easy confidence and glowing smile that made the receiver feel it was meant for her alone. But whatever did it, Chris's combination of raw physical strength and almost childlike innocence charmed them all. Dennis made Chris swear a solemn oath not to go near Melanie. Reluctantly Chris agreed. "Okay, Den-Doo, no foul. Hands off Melbo Zelbos!"

On the long ride home Chris started thinking about his own college plans. Although he had been recruited by many colleges, including Brown and Lehigh, the offer from Colgate suddenly looked ideal. He would be upstate near Dennis in the kind of countryside he had loved since Willis Reed's camp. He would be playing college basketball, which he was convinced he was ready for. He would be in an Ivy League school that carried the aura of class that he had begun to find so appealing. And with the scholarship money added to his recently achieved New York State Regents Scholarship, he would be partly relieved of the financial worries that had become almost desperate lately.

All he had to do was go back home and keep his team on their winning streak. Because if he did and that almost championship season of freshman year became a living, breathing City Championship, everything would be perfect. Chris's bubble burst when the team lost their very next game to the reigning city champs, Power Memorial High School, and then slipped deeper into a midseason slump by losing first to their archrival Xaverian, then to a strong Holy Cross team.

They won the next game convincingly

against Loughlin, but at a great price. Kevin, who had become a formidable guard with a fearsomely accurate shot, suffered a badly sprained ankle and was sidelined. In his place Coach Burke put the little spark plug Gerry O'Shea. He had spirit and courage, but at five foot six inches he was definitely little. That opening rush of seven straight victories suddenly seemed as far away as Dennis upstate at Siena.

Chris also fell into a serious academic slump in January. When he and Kevin both failed tests and were unable to produce their notebooks in advanced placement English, Mr. Perillo went to their coach. Perillo hadn't missed a game all season, but he told Burke that neither Chris or Kevin would be allowed into basketball practice until their assignments were completed. Kevin soon began to regroup academically, but Chris continued to drift. Mr. Perillo called him down to his office.

"Hey, Mr. Perillo, I got a blue card, what's up? Okay if I put these books in your closet?"

"Sure, Chris, it's your locker annex anyway, right? I should charge rent!"

Chris laughed and flopped into a chair.

Grades falling, basketball season crumbling, tuition unpaid, and he's still smiling like there's no tomorrow, thought Perillo. *What a kid.*

"What's up, Mr. Perillo? No, you don't

have to tell me, I know. My assignments are late again. I'm sorry, I'm —"

Chris Thomas at a loss for words? Perillo felt suddenly uneasy. He had planned to reprimand Chris for his poor academic performance, then give him a pep talk to encourage the better work that he was capable of. But Chris's stammer, his sudden and complete loss of his usual laughing, cocky, self-assurance worried Perillo.

"Are you okay, Chris?"

"Yeah, sure, I'm fine. It's the tuition. I don't know how Mom's going to pay it. If I could get some sort of job, I could help, but I can't find a job that I can keep and still play basketball."

"How about the Carlyle Caterers, Chris? You could pretty much make your own hours there. I know one of the partners pretty well."

"The Carlyle's right near my house. Could you really get me a job there?"

"Sure. I'll take care of it."

Perillo was so glad to see Chris smiling again that he forgot to give him the lecture on his recent poor grades. *I'll catch up with him on that tomorrow*, he thought. *He can turn it around and get A's whenever he wants with just some overnight cramming.*

Two weeks later the varsity team faced the Stanners of Molloy. Nazareth's coach Bill Burke was only in his second year, while Molloy was coached by Jack Curran, a twenty-year veteran with four City Championship trophies shining in his gym. Curran was a quiet man, respected and feared by every team that faced him, but not, it turned out, either by Burke or by Chris Thomas, aged seventeen. Chris had grown stronger, faster, and more agressive than ever. Before the night was over he had turned in a dazzling thirty-six point performance — the highest score he would never attain.

In February the time came for Nazareth's players to avenge two of their midseason losses. First they had to defeat their most spirited rival, Xaverian, for the local division crown, then Holy Cross for the leadership of the dozen teams in the league.

When Chris and his teammates charged out onto their home court for the game against Xaverian, the roar that went up from the packed gym sent the blood pumping in their veins even more than their coach's pregame pep talk. It was the biggest crowd in the school's history — almost a thousand people filling the floor bleachers and the balconies, cheering every basket, shouting for every rebound. And the team needed that shouting, for it was a fiercely contested game right to the victorious last buzzer. It wasn't as great a personal triumph for Chris as the Molloy game, but he didn't care, they won. The winning alone was sweet enough, even for Kevin who was still sidelined. But his injured ankle was definitely mending, and he was sure he would be ready for the next playoff — Nazareth vs. Holy Cross.

If Kevin had been storing up reserves of energy and fancy ball-handling, he didn't show it. His return to the lineup failed to ignite the team, and they were behind almost the entire game. Then, after one last time-out with the score tied, the magic started happening. With only six seconds left on the clock, a big hand flicked out like an ace pickpocket — Chris stole the ball! The fans roared.

Kevin Dunleavy went up with a jump shot. It was blocked. The fans moaned. Then Kevin Greaney, a fragile-looking junior with a great shot and courage to match, scooped up the ball. In one sweeping surge he laid it up perfectly. The cheering and shouting drowned out the buzzer: "Number One! Number One!"

Running off the court, Chris saw them all. His girl friend Dee beaming with joy, his mother hugging her, Mr. Perillo still clapping, and Owen smiling broadly, arms raised, index fingers pointing to the sky: "Number One! Number One! We're Number One!" Owen wouldn't be invited to the post-game party because Chris and Kevin always made a big thing about their brothers being too young to drink. But neither that nor the fact that Owen sometimes envied his brother's success changed anything. Chris was Owen's hero, and he cheered more loudly than anyone.

The party began at Elmo's house about an hour later. Chris and Dee, and Kevin and his girl friend Mary came together and were among the first to ring the bell. They were soon followed by most of the team, other friends, and many girls. Kevin swore that the number of unattached girls was growing geometrically with each win and every single one of them looked delicious. By midnight the music was getting louder, the empty beer cans were piling higher, and hands were wandering everywhere — it looked like a convention of electric eels in a sea of beer.

Then something happened. The retelling of each play of the victorious last quarter had ended. There was a quiet lull. Chris had turned to Dee in a shadowy corner of the room when Mary passed by them alone, looking for Kevin.

"Hey, Mary! Watch out — your zits are getting bigger than your boobs!"

Mary ran upstairs with tears in her eyes. Chris pulled Dee's arm and they abruptly left the party for his house. When Mary found Kevin and told him what had happened, he flew into a rage and drove to Chris's house. It was nearly one o'clock in the morning when he jumped out of his car and started ringing the Thomases' bell and pounding on the door at the same time. Dee and Mrs. Thomas ran to the front door together. When they saw Kevin they were shocked as well as frightened. Before they could get a word out, Chris's head and shoulders appeared behind them.

"Get out here, Thomas!"

"Hey, Baldy, what's —"

"Don't 'Baldy' me, you rotten bastard!"

Chris came down the four front steps. Kevin grabbed him by his shirtfront and pulled him right to his wild-eyed face. He was so angry he was snarling.

"I should kick your ass, Thomas."

"Kevin, easy does it. What'd I do, anyway?"

"You know damn well what you did. You make a rotten crack like that to my girl friend, and then you walk out like nothing happened."

"Hey, Kev, it was nothing. I was only joking."

"Joking! To you everything's a joke. Your stupid joke made her cry."

Kevin shook his friend away from him in disgust, stalked back to his car, and sped away. Chris turned slowly and looked up at his mother and Dee without uttering a word. In his eyes there was sadness and hurt — and confusion.

On Monday afternoon Mr. Perillo was surprised when Chris and Kevin came into class separately and quietly. He had expected an even more boisterous, crashing, laughing entrance than usual after Friday night's big win. But Chris just slouched in his seat, head down, his long legs fanned out on either side of the seat in front of him, while Kevin stared out the window. The class discussion was on a chapter of a book called *The Unvanquished*. Perillo's efforts to coax and badger them into discussing it failed totally. After a while Perillo was distracted by the very unprofessional wish that Thomas and Boyle would show signs of life, if only the usual notes passed with some bawdy jokes. The only note written that day he found in his book the following afternoon. Kevin must have put it there after class when Perillo wasn't looking. It read, "Mr. P., I wish you'd stop picking on me. Kevin."

That afternoon Perillo was in his office watching the activity of a small group in the park across the street. He thought he saw a small paper or envelope being passed, but he couldn't make out their faces. Chris came in so soundlessly that Perillo was startled when he turned from the window and saw him standing there in his practice uniform.

"Can I talk to you a minute?"

"Sure, Chris, just one second please." Perillo opened a loose-leaf binder that had small photographs of every student in it — some called them his mug shots — and quickly turned some pages. He jotted a name down on his memo pad and looked up at Chris.

"Nail 'em, Mr. P.?"

"I don't know, couldn't see them too clearly. It was probably nothing. This job can make you see shadows sometimes."

"You don't like this job, do you, P.?"

"It's okay, Chris, most of the time. Not always. But what about you? What's with you and Kevin? I thought you'd be on cloud nine after Friday night."

"I was. We both were, until I did something stupid."

Chris repeated the whole incident of his remark to Mary and Kevin's angry appearance at his door. Perillo listened, understanding now what accounted for the sullen disposition of both of them in class that day.

"I tried to apologize to Kevin this morning. He wouldn't even look at me. How was I supposed to know Mary would get so upset? I was only making a joke."

"Chris, you're a smart kid. You should have known that remark would hurt her feelings. Remember last fall, when I called you down after that Foley girl's mother phoned? You thought the remark you made then was just a joke, too, right?"

"But that was different. I didn't even know her. There was a lull in the party, P. I was only trying to liven things up."

"That's no excuse for what you did. Chris, there's nothing wrong with a quiet moment. You can't expect to go through your whole life flying. Even tightrope walkers have nets."

"But what do I do now? I tried to make it up to him, but he won't even look at me."

"I guess you'll have to ride this one out for a few days. You can't force forgiveness out of anyone. If Kevin still won't even listen to you in a few days, I'll have a word with him, okay?"

"Would you? Thanks a lot, Mr. P."

Suddenly a bell rang, and Chris jumped up. "Is it four o'clock already? I'll be late for practice."

"Forgetting something?" Perillo called out to Chris, who stopped and turned to face him in the doorway.

"Forget? What?"

"The girl, Chris. Don't you think you owe her an apology, too?"

"Oh, Mary? Sure. But she's not mad. She knows I was only kidding." And then the smile, a little sheepish, but with the Thomas patented glow nonetheless. On days like this Perillo welcomed that smile more than ever — it was like instant sunshine.

Three days later Mr. Perillo did have a word with Kevin. Although he had a friendly relationship with Chris and Kevin that extended beyond the classroom, Perillo was aware of an ulterior motive in his peace-making endeavor. The quarterfinal of the New York City Championship was only days away. Winning even that round would be tough enough without the spectacle of two essential players feuding. Kevin listened at-

tentively to what Mr. Perillo had to say —
his ingrained courtesy would allow no less.
He left the office quietly, cordially, and totally unmoved.

At the game on Sunday, Chris came running up to Kevin in center court for the ritual
pregame hand-slapping. Kevin kept his arms
at his side, his eyes dead ahead. Chris's ex-
uberant charge on to the court stalled out
like an old, rusted-out wreck. He traded
palms so weakly with his last three teammates that they thought he had gotten ill.

Tom Dean, Chris's co-captain, led the
team in the first half to a thirteen-point lead
over the Irish of Sacred Heart High. But it
was a deceptive spread — a fool's paradise,
as Coach Burke knew only too well. The
team was simply not playing well, a dozen-
plus turnovers in the first half proved that.
More precisely, Chris Thomas was not playing well. His famous enthusiasm had simply
vanished. Burke, knowing how much the
team needed Chris's leadership, tried to encourage him. But finally even he gave up and
put in Tim Rice in his place.

When Chris slumped down on the bench,
all his brother Owen could think of from
his seat in the bleachers was that day at the
track meet when their father returned, yelling, "What'd you do, Chris, have a heart attack!" Owen repeated the rest to himself:
Get tough, Chris. Get tough!

In the last quarter the lead evaporated to

four points. Kevin Greaney's three perfect free throws in the last minutes prevented a disaster, and the relieved Nazareth crowd roared for another victory.

What of Kevin and Chris's falling out? Kevin had a good game despite it, scoring thirteen points. Chris, however, had his poorest game of the entire season, scoring only three points before he was pulled out. Theirs was still a winning team, but with this new problem could it ever be a championship team? Not likely.

That Wednesday night in center court Kevin again refused to extend his hands to his friend. Although very few of the nearly two thousand spectators in the stands for the semifinal game against Hayes knew what was going on, Chris took it as a personal and public humiliation. It wasn't just Kevin's repeated snub that wounded him, it was also the thought, however erroneous, that all those people in the stands — whose cheers were his food and even whose jeers when he wasn't playing well were his medicine — were aware of Kevin's rejection of him. Chris could do without one or the other, but not both.

Chris played so poorly that Burke pulled him out in the first quarter. Tim Rice came in off the bench as he had in the last game, but the contest stayed close — very close. In the end Kevin Dunleavy, an excellent guard whose brother had played for Nazareth and was now in the pros, played very well, Kevin Boyle hit two shots from far out, and the game was won.

The cheering, screaming crowd had no way of knowing what Chris Thomas felt like when his winning team came off the court that night jumping and running at the same time. And, if they knew, most of them wouldn't have cared about him anyway, Chris repeated to himself.

After a quick change, the team came up out of the locker room and found seats in the stands — Chris and Kevin still far apart. All were anxious to watch the next game to find out which team they would face on Sunday in the championship game: Holy Cross, whom they had defeated for the second tier crown, or Power Memorial, with their awesome six-foot-ten-inch center Larry Petty.

When the game was over, Kevin stopped Chris on the way out of the locker room. Although he was still angry over Chris's remark to his girl friend, Kevin had begun to regret his own actions. Perhaps he was being too hard and unbending, punishing Chris for his own satisfaction, not because it did Mary any good. Besides, Kevin was truly surprised at how hard Chris had taken his friend's rejection. Kevin began to wonder if he really knew Chris after all, or if one "Baldwin Brother" could ever know what went on inside the other's heart.

"Want to go for a beer, Chris?"

"Sure, Baldy, where?" Chris couldn't believe Kevin had really asked him.

"Water's — H2O's — okay? Meet you there."

No one will ever know what the two friends said to one another that night, or if they shook hands or laughed again together. But the peace was made.

FIVE

If a kid makes the endless cuts and performs the endless drills, and sweats the endless practice of freshman, junior varsity, and varsity teams, that's usually all there is — the game, the struggle, the wonderful sport. No glory, no headlines, no college scouts. But once and forever there lives a dream — not of a winning season, not of a play-off berth, not even of a league championship, but the City Championship itself. One great game with four thousand fans and who knows how many college scouts with nationwide offers in their hands. And after that, pro ball and hints of big money, all filling the cheering air. Not for them, "Wait till next year." Their year had come. Their day was today. Sunday, March 6, 1977. The day they would remember as long as they lived. The day whose golden sun would never fade.

* * *

Among the nearly four thousand people who crowded the big university arena that day were Chris's brothers Owen and Peter, his sister Suzanne, his mother, and of course, Gramps. Kevin's brothers were all there. Those who couldn't make it this day, and who would wonder later what ever could have kept them away, began to tune in their radios for the broadcast of the game as four o'clock drew near.

"We are about six minutes away from the start of the game — both teams warming up — Nazareth to our left — Power to our right going through various drills. . . .

"They have delayed the start of the game by some fifteen minutes due to the tremendous crowds. Seats are at a premium here in the Fordham Gym — we've got people lining the rafters from one end of the gym to the other, and in just a couple of minutes we're not going to have any seats at all and they're going to be standing in the corridors. We were just informed that eleven busloads of Nazareth fans have made the trip up — eleven busloads is an awful lot of people and there are an awful lot of people in this gym. . . . It was an emotional victory for Power last week, while Nazareth sort of just pulled away from Hayes. These teams have met once before this season, in the King Tournament, and Power was the two-point victor. Wednesday, Nazareth trailed at the half to Hayes 20–19 but put together a 16–8 rift in the third quarter and then held off Hayes down the stretch. . . .

"Power has to be looked upon as the favorite, definitely, with six-foot-ten-inch Larry Petty and superguard Ed Moss. Nazareth has never won the City Championship — Power won last year. Today they could add another victory in their long string of City Championships. Everyone knows the great legends to have come out of Power, including, of course, Kareem Abdul-Jabbar. . . . Nazareth, the underdog, the Cinderella team, doesn't have the tradition. They're looking to start on that road this afternoon. So the buzzer sounds, and we'll be beginning this game in just a few moments. . . ."

The announcer's voice continued clearly across the air waves. "And now, after the introduction of the reigning champs of Power, the challengers. First out for Nazareth: No. 10, Kevin Dunleavy, brother of Mike Dunleavy of the Philadelphia 76ers, a six-foot senior guard. Next up is Kevin Boyle, No. 12 backcourt, six-foot-one-inch senior guard slapping hands with No. 14, Chris Thomas, a six-foot-four-inch senior forward. Thomas is the tallest player on this squad. No. 2: Tom Dean, a six-foot-two-inch senior guard and last, but not least, certainly, Kevin Greaney, six-foot-three-inch junior forward, No. 51. . . ."

The first two quarters were played like a weird mutation of basketball, karate, and the sixty-yard dash. There was turnover after turnover, foul after foul, fast break after stumbling fast break. If the results often looked like an ill-conceived and clumsily executed ballet, the Nazareth fans didn't care. They simply cheered louder and louder until their team ran off the court at halftime leading 26–20.

Coach Burke, however, didn't like what he saw. He was glad Chris and Kevin had patched up their differences, but the play was sloppy — the lead deceptive and perilous. He warned them against becoming overconfident only halfway through the contest, yet he could see in their eyes that they tasted victory on their sweat-salty lips.

The young coach was right. The thunderous applause that greeted their return to the court soon died away. The taste of victory turned rancid in their newly-parched throats. Power began a relentless push in the third quarter, cutting away at Nazareth's lead and spirit until, with one minute six seconds remaining, the unthinkable happened: Power tied the score 40–40 and went into a stall — forty-five seconds, fifteen seconds, seven seconds. . . .

Suddenly a quick hand whipped out and stole the ball. Kevin raced all alone ahead of the field, praying, *C'mon Chris, be there, be there when I need you. I need you now!* The emptiness — no, he was there! Oh! Fantastic Chris was there! Kevin snapped the pass, thundering feet closer and closer behind them. Chris took it flawlessly and did the "glide," his body surging up and away from the grasping arms for a climactic slam dunk at the buzzer. It was speed and reflexes and strength. It was years of practice. It was magic.

When the cheering subsided, those listening at home heard the announcer's voice again before the fourth and final quarter. "What a play! This game is everything it was cracked up to be. . . . Eight minutes to go. The City Championship in eight minutes, that's what it's come down to." Those last eight minutes, in which the score would be tied six times, would seem to take forever — and would last a lifetime. Before Nazareth went back in for the last quarter, they heard their coach's words, calm but impassioned. "We've been in tougher spots than this, right? We're a team, together we win. Now go out there and play ball!"

They went out and lost the lead for the first time in the game. The Power fans were on their feet screaming, but then the Nazareth fans raised a cheer that finally drowned them out. With five minutes remaining, Kevin Greaney came back into the game, and then Boyle went up with two free throws and tied the score 46–46. Greaney tied it again at 48–48. With one minute to go, Boyle hit two flawless free throws. It was Power 56, Nazareth 55. With twenty seconds left, four thousand fans were on their feet cheering. Chris went up with a soft, smooth, and perfect jump shot to regain the lead for his team, 57–56, but his six-foot-ten nemesis Petty came back with one point on a foul shot and tied the score again. With seven seconds left, Dunleavy faked out Petty and got fouled, putting him on the line for two free throws. He dropped the first one in — Nazareth was ahead by one. He dropped in the second as calmly as if he did this perfection every day of his life.

There were six seconds left. Power got possession. Instead of shooting immediately, they passed, and Kevin Greaney intercepted with a lightning move. There was hysteria, there was pandemonium, there was victory!

It wasn't just Owen with his arms raised high, pointing to the sky; it seemed like the whole world was shouting, "We're Number One! We're Number One!" And when Chris posed for a picture with the net draped around his shoulders like an ancient laurel wreath, he was happier than he had ever been. To seal the wonder, he had been the high scorer of the game and Kevin the Most Valuable Player. What did college matter, or scouts, or money and everyday problems — the team had won. And no matter what anyone would say, this was the fact: that what remained after all was the sweetest, most innocent, most beautiful thing of all — the winning, the glory of a City Championship for nothing but itself, at seventeen, yours forever.

This was the day they would tell their friends, old and new, about, and then their children. And when their children would one day roll their eyes and say, "Oh, Daddy, not that story again!" they would tell their friends again and wonder to themselves, *Was I really there? Was I ever so fast, so strong? Was I ever that young?*

SIX

Less than two weeks after the big game, Chris stopped by Mr. Perillo's office.

"Got a minute, Mr. P.?"

"Sure, Chris."

Chris tossed his books on the closed shelf and pulled out the gym bag that he had stowed there in his typical frenzied rush before first period. Usually he dropped his large frame into a chair with one leg hanging over the side, but this time he just pulled a chair up silently to Perillo's desk and waited.

"Well, how's it going, Chris? Still up there on cloud nine?"

"You bet your life, P.! Did you see us in the picture on the steps of City Hall?"

"I sure did. You looked very sharp — tweed jacket, turtleneck — everybody looked great. How's the job going?"

"Excellent. Ray's giving me all the hours

I can put in at the Carlyle. Thanks for the job. The money will really come in handy now with the Prom and everything coming up!"

"That's okay, Chris. I just made a phone call. You did the rest. I'm glad you're doing well there."

"Mr. P., I need your help again."

"About what, Chris?"

"My brother, Owen."

Perillo noticed that Chris's eyes seemed to cloud over suddenly and that he shifted uneasily in the chair, as if he had moved a weight from one shoulder to the other.

"Yes, I've been seeing him at the games a lot this year. How's he doing at Midwood?"

"Owen's not there anymore. He transferred to La Salle this semester, but he's been cutting out a lot."

"That's too bad, Chris. Can't you talk to him?"

"I've tried, but he's very headstrong. He thinks he's all grown-up and doesn't have to listen to anyone. I'm really worried about him."

"What does your mother think?"

"She's worried, too. I can see it in her eyes when she talks about him, but working at night makes it hard for her to keep an eye on him."

"Why did Owen pick La Salle in the first place?"

"Well, it's much smaller than Midwood,

and our friends Gregg and Billy Sullivan go there. So Mom and I thought he'd feel more at home. Owen doesn't make friends as easily as I do. He's alone a lot."

"So what happened? What went wrong?"

"I don't know exactly. Things looked good at first. Owen joined the track team and everything. Then he started cutting out of school, said he didn't belong there, that he was an outsider. He's just not happy there, P. He always wanted to come to school here with me. Mr. Perillo, do you think you could help Owen get into Nazareth in September? Mom would really be happy if he came here."

"I'm sure she would, Chris, but if Owen's been cutting school that much, he won't have enough credits to transfer. He would have to start as a freshman."

"How about summer school? Couldn't he make up some credits there? Just give him a chance. He'd be great on the track team, too. Owen's a great runner."

"Okay, Chris. I'm not in charge of admissions, but I'll look into it and see if there's something we can do."

"Thanks, P. Thanks." Chris sprang up toward the door.

"Hold on there, Mr. Thomas. Forget something — like the overdue essay?"

"I'll have it in tomorrow, I promise."

"And that incomplete you're carrying in history class?"

* * *

It was a wonderful spring that year. Big decisions, such as where to attend college, had been made and put aside — Chris was going to Colgate, Kevin to Elmira — so that the last of their high school days could be enjoyed in blissful nonsense. End-of-the-year rituals suceeded one another like pages flipping over in a photo album — Senior Breakfast, Senior Prom, Varsity Awards Dinner, Senior Awards Night, and finally Graduation Day itself.

Chris was in tremendously high spirits that day in June. When he came out of his room with his new suit on, his mother just beamed. She was always amazed that her son could spring out of the Pit looking so good, so shining and new.

They were all in the auditorium: his mother, Dee, his brothers, his sister, and Gramps. When he walked across the stage, he flashed the golden smile and accepted the maroon diploma case. But back in his seat he opened the folder and found a terrible surprise — there was no diploma inside. Chris had completed his English paper finally, but never his history essay.

After the ceremony Chris manufactured smiles for his mother's eager camera — Chris and Dee, Chris and Gramps, Chris and Kevin — holding the maroon case tightly closed in his hands. Back home, during the family graduation party, his mother insisted on having his diploma, so that it could be displayed on the mantle with his other trophies. He said, "Later, Mom . . . please," so weakly and ran upstairs so abruptly that she followed him up to the Pit.

"Chris, what is it? What's wrong?"

"Mom, I don't have a diploma."

"Don't have one? But I saw it. You carried it off the stage."

"Mom, it was empty. There was only a picture of Nazareth inside!"

Chris choked on the words. His mother saw the tears filling his eyes before he turned away from her and pounded the wall with his fists. She lifted her tiny hands instinctively to her son's shoulders, but he turned suddenly and ran past her down the stairs. He ran all the way to Kevin's house.

The party lasted most of the night. Chris laughed, made all the jokes as his friends expected, and drank steadily: first "boiler-makers" then rum combinations and "kami-kazes." By four A.M. he was protoplasm, and the company of friends decided to repay the Pie-thrower Supreme with a prank of their own. Kevin, Jughead, Sully, O'Shea, and Lubes dragged Chris into the rear of Sully's station wagon and headed down Seaview Avenue. When they got to the cemetery, they piled out and carried him in mock solemnity to a nearby monument. It was only when they laid him against the cold stone that Chris awakened, oblivious at first to his surroundings. But when he touched the headstone and realized where they had carried him, he sprang up in horror and charged after them. Just at the cemetery gate Chris stumbled and fell into a huge puddle of mud.

As the first smudges of dawn began to mark the night sky, the rowdy crew carried their falling hero back to the station wagon and headed over the bridge to the beach. Even in their condition they realized how bad Chris looked and decided that a bath in the ocean was, of course, the perfect solution.

A glorious sunrise began to light up the endless stretch of sand. The only sounds to be heard were those of the softly breaking waves, the soaring gulls, and the laughing gang of friends taking off Chris's muddied clothes. They tossed him into the welcoming arms of the ocean and dived in after him, laughing and cheering. And they couldn't have cared less that there was no one in the whole world to hear them.

Was Chris angry at his friends when he recovered from his graduation-day fiasco? Not really. He knew he had drunk too much and probably deserved getting thrown into the ocean. *It was all in fun,* he thought afterward. Everyone had enjoyed raising hell for graduation. And if there was a hint of revenge in some of the grins, he didn't notice it. As for the cemetery episode, he didn't remember it at all. If he was angry, it was at himself for having disappointed his mother so unnecessarily over an assignment he probably could have completed in an afternoon. Exactly why he had ignored the warnings at school and brought failure on himself, he never really understood.

Chris loved and needed to be the center of his friends' attention more than ever, since the basketball season had ended. Winning the championship had in one way justified to him his youthful cockiness, but in another way it created in him a need for constant reassurance that he would always be on top. Not that he was ever so deluded as to think he deserved all the glory in solitary splendor.

If he ever thought to himself that the team really needed Chris Thomas, he never let on to anyone. And when the Converse Sports Equipment Corporation named only Kevin to their "dream team" of the year's best players in the state, Chris was genuinely delighted for his friend Baldy.

July passed quickly with work and partying. Chris had become a favorite at the catering hall where he still worked because of his constant good humor and attention to the needs of his tables. With his salary and added tips he had plenty of money to go out with Dee on his nights off.

She was never really fooled by Chris's outward bravado and self-assurance. She knew his hidden fears and contradictions, knew how ironic it was, for example, that he gave her a sense of freedom from her possessive family even while he longed for some of that protective closeness himself.

Yet early in August, when Chris went away to Jack Curran's Basketball Camp in Westchester, he fell head over heels for a beautiful blond-haired girl named Beverly. Whether it was her beauty, or her rich suburban Connecticut background, Chris actually thought he was in love.

When he returned home he promptly suffered a hernia, not from falling in love with his suburban princess, and certainly not from the effort of finishing his history essay and getting his diploma, but simply from doing what came naturally — playing basketball.

He was taken for his operation to the hospital where his mother worked.

The following Saturday night, six of his band of friends, including Kevin and Sully, were denied entrance by a guard at the hospital. They left after all attempts at persuasion failed, and went partying. After midnight they decided that if they wanted to see Chris Thomas, they would in fact see him. They walked boldly through the front doors of the hospital, right into the arms of the same security guard.

"Didn't I tell you guys you weren't allowed in here?"

"But, Officer," Kevin began with his most sober intonation, "we have to get a message to his mother, Mrs. Thomas! She's a nurse in the emergency room."

"Oh, yeah? Well, you just wait here, and I'll get a message to her. Who shall I say is here?"

"Jerry Lewis — from Vegas."

As soon as the guard turned his back, the six charged up a back stairway and found Chris's room.

"Thom—ass!" called Kevin from the doorway.

Chris was so delighted at the sight of them that he almost laughed his stitches out.

"Baldy, Sully, Jughead! You guys are crazy. How did you get up here? It's almost three in the morning!"

Before they could tell Chris how they pulled off the caper, he joked to Kevin. "Hey, Baldy, they shaved all my hair for this damn hernia operation. Now I'm baldy, too!"

The guard who ran in the doorway at that moment didn't appreciate Chris's joke. He hustled the whole crowd to the elevator and out the front door. It hadn't taken Chris's mother a second to figure out what band of Jerry Lewises had come to see her son at three o'clock in the morning.

In a few short weeks they would all be separating. Sully would be off to Dayton in Ohio, Kevin to Elmira in upstate New York, and Chris to Colgate. He would be late because of the operation, but he would get there eventually.

Owen wasn't going anywhere at that point. He had taken courses in English and math that summer at Nazareth but still didn't know if they would accept him there in September as a sophomore. Although he wouldn't admit it to himself, because it was so hard to understand the war of his teenage feelings, Owen at times felt relieved that his brother would be going away. All his life he had lived in the shadow of Chris's smiling success, but as they grew older it seemed to get harder. Owen and Peter had started calling Chris "Mr. Ego" even before that championship was won, yet Owen was secretly angry at himself for being unable to catch up with him. "He just grew out of us," Owen remembered years later, "and we were jealous of him — like in 'Puff the Magic Dragon' when little Jacky all of a sudden grew up and didn't have time for Puff anymore."

SEVEN

Every year in September, thousands of students pour into hundreds of campuses across America. Cars packed with suitcases, records, plants, last year's trophies, and even teddy bears fill the parking lots. Music blares out the windows; tanned and laughing students play Frisbee or just sprawl on the grass.

Freshmen, easily identified by their darting eyes, drag suitcases up dorm stairs, nervously hoping that their parents will say good-bye downstairs in the lobby. In the ensuing days they juggle class schedules; find out what teachers have good reputations for easy grades or great lectures, preferably both; sign up for extracurricular activities; and try one last time — they hope — to get their financial aid packages straightened out. When the whirling excitement dies down they get homesick.

Chris Thomas — the handsome, intelligent, super-athlete, the personality kid — arrived alone to a quiet mid-September campus at Colgate University. His still-panting championship resounding in his ears, Chris took the stairs of East Andrews Hall two at a time up to the dorm suite he would share with three other freshmen, plus Joe Sanicola, the pint-sized valedictorian of his high school graduation class. He found his room, No. 201, completely empty. He dropped his bags, placed a picture of Dee on the barren desk, and went out into the corridor. There wasn't a living soul anywhere.

Chris shrugged at the silence and ran outside. Omens of autumn were already being felt in the rolling hills of Hamilton, New York. He slowed down and walked across the campus toward the bordering hills. Clambering to the top of one and gazing out on the valleys below, Chris remembered that first day at Willis Reed's camp. He was suddenly filled with an emotion he had never known before — a deep swelling of aching longing for the past. But the fading sun gave him little warmth, and he soon hurried down to find some companions.

A week later Chris wrote to Dennis at Siena:

* * *

Sept. 20, 1977

Dear Dennis,

What's happenin'! College ain't all it's cracked up to be. The 'gate is different from what I thought it would be. We get homework! No, I'm only kidding, it's really okay, but there is a shitload of work. I'm far behind, but in about a week I'll be caught up.

So what's going down in Albany? How is the Melbo Zelbos? . . .

The school itself is alright. There is plenty of work to do, and I really have a good schedule — Wednesday night is Party Night. The frats are really the big social life up here. We have our own Pub, but it's not like your Rat — I haven't been to either of the two bars in town yet. Things aren't that bad. . . .

There is a large supply of really beautiful girls up here, but we have a 60:40 ratio, so many of the really nice girls already have upperclassmen on a string. Women are at a definite premium. . . . I'm everyone's analyst. I've only really seen all of the freshman girls. I haven't yet seen any older ones. . . . I really don't know any of the goodlooking girls because I came up here late. They really haven't given me a fair tryout. So I intend to fix all those bitches by bringing up Bev this weekend. She should really make them take notice. Maybe they won't be so high in the ozone when they realize they're not as valuable as they would like us to think they are.

I want you to visit me soon, but not until I know some people so we won't have to sit around all night with some Handi-Wipes. The bus is only $8 — but I think it would be just as easy to hitch a ride.

If you decide to come up here and surprise me, you'll know you're in the right place when you say, "One, two, three" and everyone answers, "Squeeze!" I have all my roommates doing it.

My address is:

> Colgate U.
> P.O. Box F62
> Hamilton, N. Y. 13346

I don't have a phone. So, Den-Doo, write back and tell me what's up and give a phone # and a time to call if you can.

> *See you soon,*
> *Chris*

While waiting for an answer to his letter, Chris turned his attention to two things he was sure would lift his spirits: pledging for the Alpha Tau Omega fraternity, and starting basketball practice. With his magnetic personality Chris was a shoo-in for the frat, but his roommate Joe was very hesitant to take even the first step.

Joe was a quiet sort of guy — not weak, not afraid, just quiet. His grades were al-

ways the highest, his sense of humor ready.
And he loved to help other people. But Joe
had a self-image problem: Even with a new
pair of boots on he had trouble making five
foot six. But Chris got a hold of Joe one
night, determined to give his confidence a
boost.

"Going out for Alpha Tau, Joe?"

"Uh . . . no, I don't think so."

"Why not? It would be great for you."

"I don't think they want my type in the
frat."

"That's a lot of bull, Joe! What do you
mean, your type? You're great! You were the
class valedictorian, president of every club,
getting volunteers for everything, collecting
money for every cause. I wish I did half as
much as you."

"You really mean that?"

"I wouldn't say it, if I didn't."

"Thanks. You really think they would take
me in the frat?"

"No doubt about it. Little Joe is really Big
Joe, and it's time you believe it, because
everybody else already does! I mean it, you
have a lot to be proud of. You're as good as
anybody up here — even if you are a half-
pint!"

Chris's pep talk worked, and a week later
the Mutt and Jeff roommates became members of Alpha Tau Omega.

A week later the first basketball practice
was called by Coach Griffin. Chris, who had

lingered twenty minutes after his last class with a very pretty senior, was very late for basketball. Solution? He came roaring into the gym on a moped! When everyone, including the coach, stopped laughing, Griffin gave the team a talking to about high school being over. For openers he advised all his prospective players to show up for practice in their new Colgate shorts and T-shirts. That Friday Chris talked one of his other roommates, Pete, into going back home with him for the weekend.

Owen was home when Chris and Pete drove up. After going to summer school at Nazareth, he had been told that he would still have to start as a freshman. That's when he quit school and went to work at the Fulton Fish Market as a loader, carrying orders of iced fish to the waiting trucks from three o'clock in the morning to twelve noon the next day.

Chris knew from his mother's letter that Owen, although he wouldn't admit it, felt almost abandoned when his older brother went away to college. But it was only when Chris began to miss his family and his friends back home that he understood what his brother must be feeling. It didn't take long on that drive down from Colgate for Chris to figure out the perfect solution: He and Pete would kidnap both of his brothers and bring them back upstate after the weekend.

On Sunday, after Chris told his mother of the plan, she said good-bye and left for the hospital. Chris and Pete packed some of Owen's and his brother Peter's clothes and took them for a ride in Pete's four-speed Maverick. After a few miles there was a case of beer in the car, after another few miles they were heading over the Whitestone Bridge, away from the city.

"Where the hell are we going?" said Owen, laughing.

"You've been kidnapped, O.! Me and Pete are taking you and Peter up, up, and away!"

The red Maverick kept speeding north on the thruway at seventy-five miles per hour, while the four rowdy new companions kept opening cans of beer until Pete finally yelled, "Listen, listen, this is our radio station! 'This is Hamilton, New York, Colgate University Radio.'"

On Monday morning, Chris introduced Owen and Peter to the cafeteria personnel as his twin brothers — "new recruits" for the Colgate track team. Peter soon went off with some girls he met, and they didn't see him again for two days. On Tuesday, Chris took Owen into town for pizza. They ordered a large one. Owen had been working on weekends at a pizzeria back home, so Chris couldn't resist showing off his kid brother's new talent.

"You guys call that a large pizza? Back

home in Brooklyn that's called a pygmy pie!"

"Is that a fact! And just who is going to make a bigger one?" responded the pie-maker.

"Go ahead, O. Show him how you do it."

Owen jumped over the counter and in no time had turned the ball of dough into a veritable flying saucer. The cook couldn't believe his eyes, Chris couldn't stop laughing, and Owen's super pie was on the house.

The next day Chris left his brothers for basketball practice, after telling Owen to assemble some of his records for the Wednesday night fraternity party. Everyone on the team had followed the coach's instructions from the preceding week about wearing Colgate shorts and T's — everyone, that is, except Chris. He appeared in his Nazareth gym shorts and his Nazareth City Championship jacket. Griffin didn't laugh this time, but before he got to Chris, Mike Ferrara, one of Colgate's star players, did.

"Just who the hell do you think you are, Thomas!"

"Hey, Mikey, easy does it. What are you so heated up about?"

"The thing with the moped was funny, Thomas, but today you were a jerk. Coach said Colgate uniforms and you parade in there with your crummy high school outfit!"

"Hold it right there, Ferrara. You think you're something because you're starting for

Colgate. My team won a City Championship
— New York City, not Podunk! We won it
all!"

"That's right, Thomas, you won it all. But
that's past, your trophies mean nothing here,
nothing. You show us what you've got now,
not last year. And until you do, you're nothing. You hear me? Nothing!"

When Chris told Joe what had happened
after the practice, his voice was weak. The
self-confidence he had given his roommate
was suddenly missing in his own spirit. He
felt frightened and vulnerable.

The frat party that night was the first one
they let Chris deejay for, and he was anxious
to impress them all with his prized record
collection and stereo mixer. A disagreement
soon erupted over his choice of music — too
much James Taylor, not enough new disco
sounds, they complained. Chris grew in-
creasingly agitated when the party broke up
early, and he began piling up his records
without a word or a smile. Owen, who had
a heavy stack of records and equipment already, was starting out the door for the long
uphill walk to the dorm.

"Take this, too!" yelled Chris.

"No, you take it. All you got left is the record player."

The next thing Owen knew, a broomstick
shot past his head, missing him by an inch.
He swore at Chris and smashed his records
on the floor. The two brothers ran at one

another with fists raised and started hitting
— hard. Owen was quick, but Chris had
grown too big and powerful for him. After a
few solid punches back and forth, Owen
slipped down on one knee.

"Okay, okay. I've had enough, Chris."

"You had enough?"

"Yeah, Chris, no more," said Owen, turning away.

"Well, I didn't!" shouted Chris. He
smashed Owen so hard with an overhand
punch to the jaw that he sent him sprawling
on the floor with the taste of blood warm
and fresh in his mouth.

The next day when Chris went looking for
Owen, he found him in another frat house
where they had taken him in. He turned
away in shame, hiding his guilty hands in
his pockets, when he saw Owen's swollen
face.

"I'm sorry, O. I'm sorry. I don't know what
got into me."

"It's okay, Chris. I'm sorry, too."

"That sucker punch wasn't right, O., I'm
sorry."

"Well, I shouldn't have smashed your records, either."

"Here's some money for you and Peter to
go home. Please don't tell Mom we got into a
fight, okay?"

"No, no. I won't, Chris."

The next day Chris received a letter from
Dennis Kelly saying he would be at Colgate

by bus Monday afternoon, October 31. It was the best news he had had in a long time.

Dennis unfortunately decided to hitch-hike the one hundred and fifty miles instead. All the way from Siena to Hamilton, Dennis couldn't get more than a twenty-mile ride. Chris left his room and told Joe he was going into town to the Maroon Lounge bar to meet Dennis. That was at five o'clock. He walked across campus through the park, whose trees had now lost all their golden color, past the pond where the ducks swam together in pairs, across the road into the empty town. When he looked at his watch, Chris decided against the Maroon Lounge and flopped down on the bus stop bench. After a while the streetlight flicked on over him and the sky grew dark. Finally he heard a bus in the distance, and he jumped up as it made the turn and pulled up by the curb. An old man got off, then a cute young girl with an overnight bag — and the doors clattered shut. Chris slouched down again on the bench and zipped up his parka — it was growing cold, but he kept his lonely vigil.

Dennis finally arrived at East Andrew Hall at eight P.M. Joe told him that Chris had gone down to the Maroon Lounge two, maybe three hours before. He probably wouldn't still be there, Joe said, so he told Dennis where the fraternity Halloween party was taking place. Dennis dropped his bags and raced down the stairs two at a time. His heart told him where Chris would be. He ran across the campus and through the darkened park, past the empty pond. He came out of the park and started sprinting across the street when he saw a shadowy figure huddled under the light of the street lamp.

Chris looked up, then sprang to his feet and started running. "Den-Doo! Den-Doo!"

Chris and Dennis collided in a joyful bear hug just as Dennis shouted, "I can't believe you waited out here for three hours!" They ran to the Halloween party laughing all the way. It was three A.M. the next morning before the party broke up, and it was one wonderful reunion. Dennis would remember this day all his life. Chris would cherish it only as long as his life would allow.

EIGHT

As the cold upstate winter tightened its grip on Colgate's campus, Chris found little to cheer him as much as Dennis's visit had. For one thing, his summer love Beverly's much-heralded visit had failed to make the big impression he had expected. For another, he was getting small joy out of basketball — warming the bench was a new assignment he had little use for. And basketball was much more than a game to him. Chris loved it, he just loved playing. And now he missed it terribly. He responded, unfortunately, by cutting corners on practice and workouts, which only earned him more time on the bench. And finally, the academic demands of an Ivy League college were more than he could cram for overnight. Why was everything suddenly so hard that used to come so easily? That winter Chris started thinking that the only thing he could still do well, despite the frat fiasco of October, was to party. But just to make sure, Chris began telling girls he was twenty-one. That December he had just turned eighteen.

When Chris returned home for the Thanksgiving and Christmas breaks that year, his mother sensed an edge in his temperament that she had never noticed before. Not that he wasn't loving and concerned about her — if anything he was more affectionate than ever. But there were several occasions when she sat gazing at her oldest son, wondering about the secrets of his strong heart. And once Chris caught her at it and grew nervous and agitated. It was nothing obvious. It wasn't anything he did, but what he didn't do. There was no jesting or teasing, no wink or instantly flashing smile. Her big son was more like a little boy caught playing hookey.

In January, Mrs. Thomas rounded up Owen, Peter, Suzanne, her own brother Tom, and other family members to attend a Colgate game in New Jersey against Princeton. She was certain Chris needed some encouragement, and she was sure their presence would be the right tonic. His mother remembered how much Chris had loved it when his family and friends and teachers showed up at the high school games.

Chris desperately wanted his coach to send him in that night. He needed to show his fans from home — all seven of them — that he was still as good as when hundreds, even thousands, cheered him. The coach sent him in. Fifty-eight seconds later Chris was back on the bench — for the rest of the game. Afterward he said hello to his mother, and to Owen, Peter, Suzanne, and his two aunts and uncles. His smile was weak and false. Chris felt laid bare, humiliated, and insignificant. It was like graduation day without even the diploma case to cover his tattered pride. He was so relieved when they whistled that the bus was ready to take the team back that he actually ran to it faster than he had run in the game.

When the bus was drawing near to Colgate in the black predawn hours, Chris started wishing that it would pass right through Hamilton and keep riding north, or west, or anywhere. Anywhere else would at least be somewhere that his report card, with its string of failures, wouldn't find him.

But the bus stopped at East Andrews Hall, and the disastrous report card was lying in wait in his mailbox.

Chris Thomas was no fool. He was adrift and he knew it. What he didn't know was how to rescue himself. There were many who would gladly have gone to his aid, but how could he ask for help? Could he go back home to his mother? Go back to his high school and say, "Hello, Mr. Perillo, remember me? Remember all the laughs? Soon they may be laughing at me."

Convinced that his friends old and new,

his family, and everyone he knew only wanted him if he was the laughing, joking, big winner, Chris threw himself into that role completely. He partied relentlessly, he started telling girls he was twenty-three, he began to take off from campus without telling anyone where he was headed. He wasn't paying his dues in basketball, or in class, or in anything except the increasing hangovers.

Late in February, a reunion of Chris's high school crowd took place at Elmira College in western New York State. His old friend Kevin Boyle was in his second semester there. While he wasn't overjoyed with "the Mire," as he called it, his grades were good and he was playing basketball regularly. But winter had been so cold and miserable that he was anxious for the reunion. Sully came all the way from Dayton, Ohio, in a car he borrowed from his roommate without telling him. Jughead and Gregg hitched rides from Brockport; T.H. came from home.

Chris had told Kevin he would take the bus over from Colgate, so Kevin walked to town to wait for him at the bus stop. It was twilight, and snowing heavily, when Kevin spotted the Greyhound at the top of the hill, coming slowly down the road through the cloud of snowflakes glittering in its headlights. The bus rolled into the stop, the brakes hissed, and the door swung open.

"Hey, Baldy!" Chris shouted joyfully as he

jumped to the street in one leap, his face aglow with a true and affectionate smile.

"Hey, Thom—ass! How are ya? Glad you made it! It wouldn't be a real party without you!"

The party had already begun by the time Chris and Kevin got back to the campus. That was obvious when they opened the door and found Sully and Jughead choking one another and laughing uncontrollably at the same time. Later Chris spotted Kevin trying out his latest Don Juan routine on a cute freshman girl. As Kevin got more and more into his act, Sully picked up someone's cigar and began flicking ashes on his shoulder. Kevin was so thoroughly engrossed in his glorious quest that Sully had made a small pyre on Kevin's shoulder before Chris's explosion of laughter made Kevin spin around in a cloud of ashes. By dawn Sully was driving up the cafeteria steps with Chris and three girls inside the car and Kevin outside the car — on the hood.

By Sunday everyone had begun to head back to their own campuses or homes. Chris had told Kevin that things weren't going well at Colgate, that he was in fact thinking of taking a leave of absence. When Kevin asked what was wrong, Chris responded somewhat vaguely. "It's a lot of things, Kev. I've been hurt. I can't find time for the books. I'm trying to get in shape. I have to go and see if Mom's okay." To Kevin it sounded like nothing in particular, not just one thing to pin-point, but an avalanche of problems.

But Chris still had a great time that week-end. He laughed harder than at anytime since Dennis had come to Colgate for Halloween.

Chris noticed the large oil painting in the backseat of Sully's car when they pulled away. At that very moment, two security men were staring at the big empty space on the wall in the Mire's lobby.

NINE

When Chris went home at the end of March for spring break, his mother could plainly see that her son was in trouble. His unaccustomed silences grew longer, his laughter grew louder — and more hollow. He was nearly always nervous and edgy. But he would brush off his mother's anxious inquiries with a brusque, "It's nothing, Mom. Don't worry about me. I'm okay."

Finally, late on the last day of the vacation, she came upstairs with a basket of clean clothes and found him sitting alone in the Pit.

"It's getting late, Chris. Want me to help you pack?"

"Mom, I'm not going back."

"But today's Sunday, Chris. Don't you have classes tomorrow?"

"Mom, I said I'm not going back. I'm leaving Colgate."

Mrs. Thomas was so stunned that she just sagged down on the edge of the bed next to him with the fresh clothes piled in her lap.

"Chris, what's wrong? Tell me. I love you."

"Mom, it's everything! My grades are terrible. I didn't do anything in basketball all season. I let you down. I made all the wrong friends — they're not my friends. I don't have any friends up there, Mom. Do you hear me? I don't have any friends!"

And then it happened. Chris began to cry, not little tears but bitter sobs. His mother reached over to him to hold tight his shaking, caved-in shoulders. And as she did, the neat pile of fresh, clean clothes spilled over into a ragged heap at her feet.

Chris did return to Colgate after the spring break, but only to begin the odd ritual of dismantling a dream. Over the next few weeks he slowly packed some things and discarded many others. Among the last possessions he placed in his gym bag was the picture of Dee he had kept on his desk — the one thing that had not changed all year. If anything he only loved her more.

Spring had arrived in Hamilton in all its beautiful and indifferent innocence, though Chris scarcely noticed or cared as he crossed the campus and circled the pond on his way down to the bus stop. Time had become unhitched — like a damaged trailer abandoned on a lonely country road.

* * *

In June of that year, Mrs. Thomas, thinking that a change of scenery would help her
son sort out the muddled pieces of his life,
suggested he go out to the country and stay
with his father for a while. Chris's father
had remarried years before and moved to
Easthampton with his new wife and her
children. Chris was reluctant at first, saying
that he didn't want to leave her alone and
that his brother Peter was already out there.
But his mother reminded him that Owen
would be home with her and convinced him
to go out to the Hamptons.

The Hamptons is a dreamy summer place
two hours east of New York City on the
south shore of Long Island. Like resort areas
near many other American cities, it is popu-
lated by the rich in their guarded estates by
the sea, by vacationers in rented bungalows,
by college kids looking for summer jobs and
a good tan, and, finally, by those who live and
work in the towns all year-round.

Mr. Thomas, following in the steps of his
father and grandfather, had gone into the
fish business. By the time Chris arrived at the
shingled house with the white shutters that
they rented near the store, his father had
expanded his business. There was now a
store, a small restaurant and bar, and a patio
— all called Eastern Seafood.

Chris, age eighteen, was very impressed
when he made the turn from the country

highway on to Main Street. The large shingled houses sheltered by enormous elm trees, the windmill atop the hill overlooking the still pond, the expensive shops with even more expensive cars parked outside — it was a long, long way from where he had grown up in Brooklyn. *Not bad*, Chris thought to himself, *not bad at all!* And he hadn't even yet seen the estates spilling off Lazy Pond Lane and over the quiet green hills to the sea below.

Chris tried to take Easthampton by storm. But the citadels of wealth do not yield to every attacker, no matter how clever, how handsome, or how determined. He noted how the rich dressed and how they spoke. These things were superficial and easily imitated, he thought, but there was no imitating money — you either had it, or you didn't. And Chris Thomas definitely did not have it.

Chris began to work at his father's store, but his earnings did not go very far with the new friends he had begun to make — beautiful suntanned girls, twenty-eight-year-old guys with Rolex watches and purring foreign sports cars.

As always, his good looks and sunny personality had made the first step, making friends, easy. But keeping friends, which he had come to equate with impressing them, was becoming an obsession with him. Chris began to accept as a fact what was never true in the first place: that two years before, people had crowded around him only because he was some sort of hero to them — because he impressed them.

But impressing this new crowd was another matter. Chris would grow angry and frustrated when he had to make up excuses and beg off because the crowd was heading for someone's beach club or to a restaurant or nightclub that he couldn't afford: *Who do they think they are! They're like a pack of Mike Ferraras from Colgate, telling me I can't cut it — I'm not good enough.*

One day he was surprised at work by one of his new friends, Sandy Thompson. Chris didn't really care for him; he thought Sandy a little too slick, but he *was* welcome in all the right places with all the right people.

"Chris Thomas! What are you doing here?"

"How ya doing, Sandy! Uh, I'm helping out. This is my father's store."

"Is that right. Well, good luck to you. Coming to the beach later?"

"Yes, sure, I'll be there."

That afternoon at the beach, when everyone else had gone into the ocean for a swim, Sandy began the conversation.

"Like working at that store, Chris?"

"It's okay, I guess."

"Make much money there?"

"No, are you kidding? But my pop needed some help. He's been very busy."

"How would you like to make some real money?"

"Doing what?"

"Well, let's just say for now that I am into a new business venture. A guy like you could do very well in the fast lane. If you're interested in real dollars, you get in touch, okay?"

Chris met with Sandy a few days later, on Thursday. When he learned that Sandy's "business venture" included computer fraud with other people's bank accounts, Chris felt strangely like a little kid whose friends had all suddenly started shaving. On Friday he went back home to see his mother, depressed by his new-found knowledge of the facts of life, and convinced that there had to be a better way to make some money. While he was home, he got calls from Dennis and Kevin. On Saturday Chris and Kevin went out. Dennis couldn't make it that night but promised Chris he would see him in the Hamptons in July. The evening ended early. Dee was away with her family, there were few girls around the bar, and Chris seemed out of sorts. Kevin tried to joke and lift his spirits, but kidding Chris about all the weight he had put on wasn't the right move — Chris finished his beer and walked out.

That would be the last time Kevin would see his friend for almost a year. Kevin had decided not to return to Elmira in September but instead to head west across America with his old friend T.H. Kevin had a name for his journey — he called it his "odyssey." If settling in California and finishing college at Berkeley was the end of the odyssey, fine. If not, then the journey itself, he hoped, would be education enough.

Chris had embarked upon his own odyssey, but it was a circle — between home and the Hamptons. In July, as he promised, Dennis drove out to Easthampton to see Chris. When they met, his first reaction was a fleeting, half-felt hurt at not being greeted with a happy shout of "Den-Doo! Den-Doo!" He brushed that thought aside quickly, but not his shock at Chris's size. He had gained twenty-five pounds, Dennis thought. And with an ache of nostalgia he remembered the joyful time at Siena College when they had played ball with his huge roommate Mark, and Chris kept laughing and shouting, "Give it to 'the house!' Give it to 'the house!' "

That night they went out to the Boardy Barn in Westhampton for some "grub and grog." Dennis had worked hard all week and was really up for a good time, but the evening never got off the ground. It wasn't because of the place — there were beautiful girls, great music, and even "Dishwater Dogs" when you got hungry. Everybody seemed to know Chris there. They waved and said hello and sent over drinks, gestures he was able to return only one for three. Chris seemed very distant to Dennis, almost in another world. Dennis tried to reach out to him; he knew his friend was troubled.

"Chris, you want to talk about it?"

"What? Talk about what?"

"I don't know. You seem upset, you're not yourself."

"Not to worry, Den-Doo, not to worry. This is the real me, all two hundred and twenty pounds."

"Is it that basketball didn't work out for you at Colgate? I know what that's like, believe me, Chris. When I got cut at Siena, I found it very hard to take. They told me I was obsessed with playing. And I was, too. It was my dream."

"It's everything; everything's wrong," was all Chris answered.

So Dennis left him alone. He accepted the brush-off, thinking to himself, *Well, I've had my times, too, when I didn't want to talk to anybody and I just wanted to be by myself, so maybe that's what Chris needs.*

"Want to go home, Chris?"

"Yeah, sure, let's get out of here."

In the parking lot, Chris had just turned on the ignition when a black Corvette screeched out of a parking spot in reverse. Although it came within inches, it didn't hit Chris's car, but he started yelling obscenities out his window anyway.

"Chris, take it easy. It's not worth it," said Dennis, trying to calm him down. But when Chris shouted again, the Corvette's doors opened, and out came two men ready to fight. Chris reached underneath his seat and in an instant charged out of his car with a tire iron flailing above his head.

"Chris! What are you, crazy?" shouted Dennis, jumping out of his side of the car. At the sight of Chris waving a tire iron and yelling, "C'mon, you morons, c'mon. I'll take both of you on right now!" the two men looked at one another, got back in their car, and drove away. Chris flung the tire iron after them, then jumped into his car and sped away after them into the darkness. He left Dennis just standing there dumbfounded.

For twenty minutes Dennis waited under the lamppost, chilled by the ocean breeze blowing across the lot. He was sure Chris would come back. He did, and they drove back home in silence.

Late that September, Mr. Perillo's phone rang at school.

"Mr. P., it's me, Chris."

"Well, how are you! How've you been?"

"Fine, great. Did you have lunch yet?"

"Yes, but what . . ."

"Mind if I come over for awhile?"

"No, great. Come right over."

Chris came bounding in the door ten minutes later, carrying a small package. He had lost most of the weight he had gained, and with a tan and the famous smile flashing

Perillo thought he looked great. They shook hands, and Chris held out the package.

"What's this?"

"Scallops, P. Bay scallops. The real thing, not the ocean scallops they stamp out and pass off as Bays. I got them this morning before I left the Hamptons."

And there, to Perillo's surprise, inside the plastic container were several pounds of scallops on ice.

"Thanks, but you didn't have to bring anything, just yourself."

"Well, it's sort of a peace offering. I know I've really been out of touch."

"C'mon, sit down. This is like old times. What are you doing now? I know you left Colgate. Things weren't what you thought they would be up there?"

"No, it was a lot different. After senior year here, I thought I was on top of the world. Everything was so great. I wanted it to stay that way forever. But it didn't."

"It takes a while to adjust to a new place. Did you give it your best shot?"

"I just didn't fit in up there. I didn't belong. Nobody seemed to know me anymore."

"It's funny, Chris, but I felt a little like that when you guys left here. Those were great days — we had a lot of laughs. We had some problems, too, but we worked things out. I told Kevin I probably should have left when you guys did. Things have never been the same."

"You're not thinking of leaving, are you, P.? I know Coach Burke has pulled out and Mr. Settanni and —"

"A lot, Chris, have either gone or are going. There's too much politics around here, too much cynicism. But forget about me, let's hear about you."

And Chris told him. For a hour or more, he told him how wonderful that championship spring really was — like a flirtation with immortality. And then he talked about Colgate and sitting out most of the basketball season on the bench, about classes he cut and assignments he missed, about friends he made who weren't like his old ones, and about coming home finally to what he was sure was an "unwelcoming committee," no matter what people said. He thought he shouldn't even visit his old high school, because he had failed and disappointed everyone. Perillo didn't think Chris really believed him when he insisted that that wasn't true.

Their talk that day ended on a more optimistic and hopeful note: Mr. Perillo encouraging Chris to make a new start and return to college, Chris agreeing that that was a good idea and promising that he would apply to C.W. Post. Its campus lay halfway between home and the Hamptons. On the way out, Perillo stopped Chris.

"How's Owen doing, Chris?"

"He's good, real good. He's working full time at T & C."

"T & C?"

"You know, in the fish market. He's still a loader, but he'll have his own stall someday, I'm sure he will."

Perillo thought Chris left that day in good spirits. He was certainly smiling as broadly when he left as when he had come in. Several teachers, having heard he was in the building, stopped by to say hello. What was said in between these interruptions was for the best, Perillo thought; getting things out in the open made them easier to deal with. Perillo thought Chris had told him everything. He was wrong.

Through that fall and winter Chris split his time between his mother's house in Brooklyn and his father's in Easthampton. Owen continued to live at home with his mother and work every night from three A.M. to twelve noon the next day at the market. He thought about returning to school sometimes, but the memory of past disappointments kept such thoughts from ever becoming reality.

When the spring came, Mrs. Thomas had an opportunity to go to Scandinavia with the nurses' association of her hospital. Her daughter Suzanne was fast becoming a very pretty young woman, and Mrs. Thomas had begun to feel that perhaps too much of her energy had been taken up by her sons at the expense of her little girl. She tried to put aside her worries about her sons being in their neighborhood, which had been the scene of much trouble and tension recently. She hoped the boys' nearby grandfather would be able to keep an eye on them. Just this once she needed a little holiday.

The European trip Mrs. Thomas enjoyed with the other nurses and Suzanne was everything she hoped it would be. But she came back home to a double shock. First she learned that Owen had gotten into a fight with two men. He stood his ground like his father used to tell him: "If you know you're right, don't back down, don't be a wimp and put your tail between your legs and split." Owen didn't split, but his scalp did when one of his foes got him from behind with a bat. His father had told him something else: "You can't be stupid. You can't make too many mistakes." This mistake cost him ten stitches in the head. Next, Mrs. Thomas was told how Peter, who had left the Hamptons to live with her again, had taken on some of the neighborhood toughs. Peter and his three friends had done such a good job that he was sent back out to his father's house until things cooled off. Mrs. Thomas, that most gentle of creatures, wondered if she would ever have a normal day again.

TEN

Chris had begun to spend more and more time in the Hamptons during that spring of 1979, and less and less time with his old friends. Even Kevin, who had returned from his California odyssey bruised but unbroken, saw Chris only if he initiated the get-together with a phone call. Dennis, who had grown bitter over Chris's seeming rejection of him, thought sadly to himself, *Did Chris think because I saw he had clay feet like everybody else, that I didn't love him? I just tried to reach out, but he was in another world.*

In some ways things seemed to be looking up in Chris's new world. He had just gotten a beautiful new silver van with plush rust-and-gold upholstery and carpeting, a built-in stereo tape deck, and every conceivable option. It was loaded — and Chris was burdened with a huge loan to repay.

His father, meanwhile, had expanded the

seafood restaurant in Easthampton and bought a new house. Owen came out one weekend, and all three brothers helped their father with the moving. Chris didn't stay for long in the new house. He said he wanted some privacy and moved into a rented mobile home in a neighboring town.

For most of that summer Chris worked as the day manager of the restaurant, making sure that all the different fish on the menu were in fresh supply, checking the orders of canned goods, making sure the waitresses were on time, the liquor was ordered, the linens and silver and glassware were clean. It was a big responsibility for a nineteen-year-old, but no one paid much attention when he disappeared for two or three days at a time.

That summer, Owen began to commute weekly to the Hamptons. He worked two days a week for his father and pretty much kept to himself. While Chris was spending more time at work every day with his father, Owen would say, "Hi, Pop, how are you doing?" and go out fishing by himself, or if the weather turned bad, he would just stay home alone.

In August, after returning from one of his unannounced trips in his van, Chris walked up to his trailer door and turned the key. It didn't work. He held the key up and squinted at it in the dim moonlight. It was the right key, all right. Then he looked back at the lock and realized how shiny it was — somebody had changed it. He ran to the nearby house where the manager of the trailers lived and pounded on his door until the old man appeared at the window.

"Who the hell changed the lock on my trailer?" he shouted.

"Just quiet down there, boy. I changed it. I don't want you and those friends of yours coming around here anymore."

"I pay my rent! It's mine. I live there!"

"Not anymore. It's the end of the month. Just don't bother sending next month's rent."

"But my stuff is in there! You can't do this to me!"

"Oh, yes, I can. Come back for your things in the morning. Now get out of here before I call the police."

Chris drove away in a rage and slept in his van that night at the end of a deserted road. He was thankful for the feeble moonlight coming through his windshield, for he had grown afraid of the dark.

In September Chris enrolled at C.W. Post College. He had hoped to try out for their basketball team, and the coach promised to try to get a room in the dorms for him. It wasn't Colgate, and it was a three-hour ride every day back and forth, yet it was a step in the right direction. But they couldn't arrange a room for him on campus until January, and Chris could see that he wouldn't be able to get in shape for basketball on time.

Those twenty-five pounds he had put on again had really slowed him down. By the first week in October he stopped going.

That same week there was a fire in his father's restaurant. They thought it must have started in the kitchen, but no one could tell for sure. By the time it was over, Eastern Seafood was a smoldering pile of rubble.

On Thursday in the third week of that month, Mr. Perillo's secretary told him he had a visitor. When he looked up from his desk he saw Chris filling the doorway.

"Chris Thomas! It's good to see you. God, it's been a long time!" said Perillo, coming around the desk to greet him and shake hands. "C'mon, pull up a chair. This is a real surprise."

"Well, I meant to call, but I've been running around a lot. So I figured I'd just surprise you and come right in."

"Well, I'm glad you did. How's your mom and Owen?"

"Fine. They're both doing fine."

"And how about you? I see you gained some weight. Did you start at C.W. Post?"

"Yeah, P., I did. But, well, that's what I wanted to talk to you about."

"Sure, let's go outside. This place is getting to me today."

They walked out through the front doors that Perillo had first entered almost fifteen years before, and down the broad front steps that Chris had first climbed with Kevin under the fire scaffolding six years before. They walked slowly under the fading trees, around the building, and then around again. Chris did most of the talking. Perillo soon realized that he had a lot on his mind, so he just listened while Chris went over the past year of his life, sometimes reaching back two years into the past.

When they made yet another turn past the parking lot, Chris stopped. "Hey, P., c'mon have a look at my van!"

Chris brought Perillo to his silver van gleaming in the lot. After showing him some of the gadgets and accessories he had installed, Chris pulled out a packet of photographs he had taken in the Hamptons, and he and Perillo sat on the open doorway of the van to look at them. There were some of an attractive blond named Sharon — not a young girl, Perillo thought, but pretty. There was one of Chris driving his van, taken from the passenger seat, probably by Sharon. And there were many beautiful pictures of sunsets, some taken across limitless miles of ocean, others through the barren trees of winter in Easthampton.

"P., I want my youth back."

The simple, eloquent desperation of the statement stunned Perillo. He looked at Chris sitting just two feet away, and in the youth's confused and frightened eyes thought he was looking across the years at every kid who ever brought his troubles into his office — all the pain of drunken fathers, hysterical mothers, overbearing teachers, sexual terrors and unwanted pregnancies, drugs and violence, and despair. Perillo had coped with these things — these troubled students were still a minority, he usually rationalized to himself. But he wasn't prepared to see that all-too-familiar look in the eyes of Chris Thomas.

"I don't understand, Chris. You're only nineteen. You have your whole life ahead of you."

"I've made a mess of it. I've got to get away from the Hamptons, from all those people. They're too old for me."

"How did you get involved with that crowd?"

"I thought they were something. I was impressed with all the money and the fast talk. Dennis tried to tell me, but I wouldn't listen. I thought they were my friends. But all they want is what they can get out of you. They pat you on the back all the time; sure, they're just trying to find out where they can break it."

"You can change, Chris. Forget the past. Don't be so down on yourself."

"Do you really think I can change?"

"Of course you can. Changing isn't hard, choosing to change is. You have to make a choice, you have to decide that you are worth it. You have to believe in yourself enough to pay the price."

"I never thought about believing in myself — it was automatic. It was so automatic that I didn't know it was gone until I had lost it. I was never as confident as people thought, I only put it on half the time because I thought I had to impress people. I thought they wouldn't love me if I was afraid or if I didn't make them laugh."

"Then you'll need courage now to choose."

"I don't know if I have it."

"You do. You do."

"You talk as though you've had to make some choices, too."

"I have. And if I can change, you sure can."

"Are you going to leave Naz High, Mr. P.?"

"Yes. You know your old coach Bill Burke is gone. Marty Harrison has replaced him. I've been out on interviews this month. Looks like we both have a new life ahead of us."

"I don't think I should go back to Colgate. It wasn't the right place for me. I was thinking of going to Colorado or else maybe somewhere nearby and staying home for a while."

"Well, if you really want to get away from your Hampton friends it doesn't make sense to go to Colorado, right? You said some of them are heading out there. Where would you go closer to home?"

"I'm not sure, maybe Fordham or Manhattan. Maybe Coach Harrison can help me get some interviews."

Suddenly the end-of-the-day school bell rang out across the parking lot. Mr. Perillo automatically looked at his watch. "Hey, Chris, it's two-thirty! We've been talking for two hours! I have to get back inside."

"You really think I can start over again?"

"No doubt about it. I believe in you. Have faith."

"Thanks."

"Okay, let's go."

"Wait one second." Chris reached back inside his van and pulled out the photograph of himself driving, looking out through the large windshield of his beloved silver van. "I want you to have this, P."

They walked together back inside the building but separated when they got to Perillo's office.

"See you later." Chris smiled and disappeared into the crowds of students in the corridor. Mr. Perillo walked alone into his office. He was usually happy when students came back to say hello, but now he was deeply disquieted — he felt worn out. He had given Chris everything he had. Maybe he just didn't have it anymore. He listened completely, he tried to use his intelligence, he tried to share his heart. But this wasn't supposed to happen. Not to this one. Not Chris Thomas, that luminous kid from so few years past — he couldn't be in this kind of trouble, beyond help, beyond saving. It just wasn't possible.

That afternoon when Chris came home, his mother was delighted to see him.

"Hi, Mom!"

"Chris! What a surprise. I'm so glad you're home again."

"I'll double your food bill."

"So what?" Mrs. Thomas smiled. "I don't know a better way to spend money."

"Where's Owen?"

"Upstairs sleeping. He only got home from work a couple of hours ago."

"How's Dee doing at the hospital?"

"Oh, just fine. She's going to be a terrific nurse. Did you talk to her today?"

"Not yet. I'll call her in a minute. Think you can put up with me at home again?"

"Of course I can! What kind of a thing is that to say!"

"I'm leaving the Hamptons — for good this time, Mom. I'm going back to college."

"That's wonderful! I'm so happy. I really am." And she ran over to her son and hugged him as tightly as she could, smiling the same smile she had lavished on him at birth and bequeathed to him as the finest of all gifts.

Chris called Dee to go out together that night, but she was going on duty for the four P.M. shift at the hospital. So they postponed getting together until Friday. After dinner he called Kevin.

"Hey, Baldy, what's up?"

"Long time no hear. Where are you?"

"I'm home. How about tossing down a few at H2O's?"

"No more H2O's, Thomas; it closed two months ago. People hang out at the Last Hurrah these days."

"Okay, Baldy. Me and Owen will meet you there about nine."

Chris, Owen, and Kevin were just about the only ones who did meet there that night — the place was nearly deserted. After a few beers and questions about where everybody was, Kevin noticed that Chris seemed to grow distant.

"Hey, Thom—ass, everything okay?"

"Oh, sure, sure. I'm coming home, going back to college, I hope."

"When? In January?"

"Hope so. I'm going back to the Hamptons once more. We're still cleaning up after the fire. I have to make some more money for tuition, if I can. Then it's back home for keeps."

After a few minutes of near-silence, Owen suggested they try the Night Owl. But Chris said he was tired and didn't feel too well. So the night at the Last Hurrah ended quietly not long after it began.

The next day Chris was sick and stayed home. He called Dee, who came over to be with him for most of the afternoon. When Chris told her about his hopes to return to college and start all over again, she was as happy as his mother had been. Before she left, she even tried to talk him out of going back to the Hamptons at all, but he promised her it would only be for a short time.

"Don't be long. You know I love you."

"Love you, too."

Chris left the next day for Easthampton and arrived late in the afternoon at his father's house, where he had been living along with his brother Peter since getting locked out of his mobile home. For the next few days he helped with the postfire cleanup, but otherwise kept to himself. The nights he spent sorting out things that had piled up in his room, deciding what he would discard and what he would bring home with him. He tried to get rid of everything that reminded him of the last two years: empty champagne bottles, empty beer bottles, tapes, photographs, useless keys to doors he had forgotten. The room actually looked neat when he finished, not like his Pit back home at all.

Wednesday night was Halloween — the night of witches and devils — party time before the onset of the long winter. Chris got into his van and drove to town, past that still pond, down Ocean Avenue and to the beach, where he got out and walked across the sand to the water's edge. The moon, nearly full now, cast a soft and pallid light upon the fine planes of his face and upon the dark arms of the sea. He looked up at the stars glowing so bravely all alone way out there in space. He felt at peace.

Then thoughts of other nights and other places came in like the waves before him. And the thought of another Halloween night — was it only two years ago? — when Den-Doo got off that bus and he was so happy after his lonely three-hour wait under the street lamp. He longed for companions like the friends he used to have.

Chris climbed back into his van and drove away from Easthampton, down the deserted county highway for miles, until he spotted what he mistook for a friend's car parked outside a seedy, local gathering place called Wildflowers. There was no one he knew inside, but he ordered a beer and after awhile began a game of darts, shooting perfectly at the board that under the low-beamed ceiling seemed lost in a wall of dusty trophies.

Someone came in around one A.M. who recognized Chris, not one of the Easthampton summer crowd, but a local, a "barnacle." At his side was a woman named Dierdre, attractive, older, with a few gray streaks in her dark hair. When Chris heard his name called out, he turned suddenly and banged his head against a low beam. Dierdre and the barnacle thought Chris looked a little dazed, but he shook it off and stayed another half hour with his only companions. Finally he left by himself and headed back to East-hampton. Without telling him, Dierdre followed in her car.

One mile down from Wildflowers, the road curves sharply to the left. At three A.M. a woman called the police and said she had just heard a terrible crash. Dierdre made the turn on that deserted highway and saw a silver van crumpled against a tree. Sprawled out by its side was Chris. Dierdre ran back to her car and drove away — she drove away, as his blood, clear and bright, flowed out of him into the sand. The police came, then the ambulance and the doctors. But not all the doctors in the world, not all the prayers, not all the love on this earth could save Chris Thomas now — he was gone forever.

ELEVEN

Even as his brother lay dying, Owen, unaware of the tragedy, went to work as usual at the fish markets. He liked it best in those predawn hours because it was nice and quiet. Many of the stalls weren't even open yet as he passed, smiling and happy. But as he began to see some of the other workers there, he slowed down. First he thought he was imagining things, but then he felt sure they were looking at him in a funny way. He stopped one of his friends.

"What's going on around here, Joey?"

"You don't know?"

"Know what?"

"I ain't gonna tell you," said Joey, turning away.

"No, come over here."

"Your brother Chris was in an accident."

"My brother?" said Owen, moving toward the food wagon for some coffee. "No, he's probably all right. You can't stop him, no how."

Joey's son passed the coffee to Owen and asked, "How are ya feelin'?"

Owen laughed. "Fine. What do you mean?"

"How could you laugh?"

Owen put his coffee down. "What are you talking about?"

"Go see Jimmy Cunningham."

When Owen asked him, he said, "Go call your mother, no, I mean call your father's house. Use the phone in my office."

Owen's brother Peter answered the phone in Easthampton — in ten seconds it was over. Owen flung the phone off the desk, then kicked a chair over and ran outside, shoving people and wooden crates away as he ran, half-crazed with grief, down the center of the market. Finally his boss tackled him and pulled him aside. When Owen stopped sobbing, his boss, still holding him, said, "You have to go tell your mother. She's still at work at the hospital, right? I'll drive you over."

Owen found his mother in the crowded and noisy emergency room. When Mrs. Thomas saw Owen standing there, she thought he had gotten hurt at work.

"What's the matter, Owen?"

"You gotta come here. I gotta talk to you," he said, pulling her gently into one of the little side rooms.

"What . . . what is it?"

"Take it easy. Here, sit down."

"No, tell me what it is."

So she took it standing up — "Chris died. He got killed in a car accident" — and then her legs gave out underneath her, and she cried out simply, "No, no, no," and Owen held her tightly as she cried. It was the hardest thing he had ever had to do in his whole life — when he said those words it was like he was making his own brother die.

The phone rang at Kevin's house at eight-twenty that morning. Kevin thought nothing of hearing Owen's voice, he figured there was a message from Chris; but the news was Owen's to give. "Chris is dead, he was killed last night in a car accident." Kevin froze. He saw his father's image from long ago, and Chris's face the way it looked that first time they met at the armory. And in that moment what he loved was all in the past. He couldn't speak.

"Kevin, are you there? Are you okay?"

"Yes. Okay. I'll come over."

Kevin walked out of his house without telling anyone the news he had just received. When he got there, Mrs. Thomas, mercifully occupied with the busyness of death, told him he had to break the news to Dee. So he left to borrow a car from Sully's parents and came back for Owen.

They found Dee finally in the nurses' cafeteria. She was overjoyed at first to see them, but then, wondering exactly why Kevin and Owen were there at that hour, she put the question to them with the simple courage of women everywhere. Kevin tried but could not force an answer out of his heart. It was left to Owen again to say those three words, like he would for the next two days. "Chris is dead" . . . "Chris is dead" . . . "My brother is dead."

Mr. Perillo's phone rang about one P.M. at home that day — he was playing faculty hookey.

"Kevin Boyle! How are ya?"

"I'm okay, but . . . I have some bad news."

"Oh? What is it?"

"It's really bad."

"Kevin, what is it? What's happened?"

"It's really bad."

Perillo knew at that moment it was something beyond telling, something so terrible that Kevin could not utter it. "Just tell me who it is . . . just who."

"It's Chris."

"Chris, your brother?"

"Chris Thomas."

"How bad is it?"

"He's dead. Chris is dead."

"No, oh, no, not him. I just saw him. What happened?"

"A car accident in the Hamptons — he died instantly."

"The Hamptons? But he came home."

"No, he went back again Monday. Would you make some calls?"

"Yes, tell me who."

"Let them know at school."

"Yes, I'll tell your friend Mr. Reiter."

"And call Settanni, too. And Burke, and anyone else who has to know."

Perillo began to make the calls, hearing his own voice as though it were someone else's, far away. One of his calls was to Tom Dean, Chris's co-captain on their championship team. Tom called Dennis Kelly at Siena. It was a brief call. Dennis thought Tom was simply returning the one he made to him over Labor Day weekend. But Tom had something else to say.

"Look, I got something to tell you . . ."

Dreams die so easily by phone. Dennis packed his bags and headed home.

Perillo met Kevin that night at his house. There were about a dozen people there at first, but Kevin and Perillo drove alone to the house of the teacher who had first introduced the Baldwin Brothers to Perillo six years before. They sat for hours in Mr. Settanni's living room while his two-year-old son laughed and tumbled on the rug. Perillo couldn't stop the thought that kept coming into his head: *Why does he laugh so much, doesn't he know what's happened?"*

By Friday it seemed that everyone knew that Chris Thomas was dead. They came

from everywhere to pay their respects —
from Ohio, Massachusetts, Maryland, and
Connecticut. They came from the block he
grew up on near St. Vinnie's and from far
out on Long Island to see their fallen hero.
There were girls who saw him from a distance and longed in their lonely rooms to
know him more; there were guys who knew
him only because he was the right one to
know for the last two years. There were the
friends who enjoyed his casual grace. And
finally there were those few who loved him
— those who were fortunate enough or naive
enough; those who were brave enough or true
enough.

Most of them who came to say good-bye
that day had no experience with tears. Some
had cried because they were cut from a team
when they were fourteen, or because they
hoped desperately to be asked to a party and
were left behind. Some, like Dennis and
Kevin, had wept for their fathers before their
time. But sorrow is a poor teacher. Those
earlier deaths did not begin to tutor them
for this death of youth. And there were those
like Perillo, who didn't know how much he
had lost until Chris was gone. He wept bit-
terly and cursed all the kids that he knew
had lied and cheated and broken their parents' hearts and repaid their teachers' con-
cern with mockery and indifference. "Why
not them?" he repeated. "Why not them?"
And Kevin sat alone, calling out faintly to his

lost friend — "Thom–ass . . . Thom–ass" — smiling already at the remembrance, denying the certainty that Chris would never answer. Dee stayed by Mrs. Thomas's side, brave and steady and unblinking.

The day and night passed, marked by the simple little ways that people deal with their greatest tragedies — the touched hand, the frightened embrace, the patted back, the silent look into wasted eyes, the fingers soft against the ruined cheek.

In the morning, after the service, they left Chris in a tiny chapel, protected from the steady rain, unburied because he had died too fast even for the gravediggers. His heart had come to know peace, but it had not yet grown accustomed to silence.

Owen walked away beside his mother past the aging tombstones, the words of a song he had half-forgotten echoing in his memory: "Little Jacky Paper loved that rascal Puff." That magic dragon. Owen held his mother tightly.

"Dragons live forever but not so little boys."

TWELVE

When Owen returned to work at the market, nothing seemed familiar anymore. Perhaps he just never noticed it before, but it was an ugly building. Even the color they had painted it to try to make it look better reminded him of the fish they couldn't sell and had to throw away. The streets were filthy; fish heads rotted in the gutters. When he walked inside, past the stalls where everyone looked funny at him two weeks before, he knew he couldn't stay there.

Owen went out to Easthampton at the end of November, as soon as his younger brother Peter returned home to stay with their mother. There was still much work to be done rebuilding the restaurant after the fire that had taken place early in October. That kept Owen so busy during the day and so tired at night that he would soon fall asleep, instead of staring at the ceiling thinking of his lost brother.

When Owen did want to go out again at night, his father told him he had to be home by ten.

"What are you talking about? Ten o'clock? I'm eighteen years old."

"I don't care how old you are! You can't drive after dark no more. No one's driving after dark in this house anymore."

But, after Christmas, when Owen returned from his mother's house, enough work had been completed on the fish store to reopen it for business, while work continued on the restaurant. Owen was released from his curfew, perhaps more completely than he wanted. Every night, in the middle of the night when it was the darkest, he would have to climb into his brown Dodge Tradesman van and head west, driving two hours alone on the deserted highways. Sometime before dawn he would make it to the Fulton Fish Market, buy the supplies for the day, and head back to the Hamptons, driving east into the rising sun.

In April, Owen came back to his mother's house for a few days so that he would be with her for the big party. Some friends of Chris's had organized a reunion that would also begin a memorial for the friend they missed so much. The Last Hurrah wasn't empty that night, the way it was when Owen went there in October with Chris and Kevin.

The place, closed to the public, was soon crowded with almost three hundred people. The noise and the music went on through the night. Mrs. Thomas and Owen were just as glad that so many came and hadn't forgotten as they were for the thousands of dollars that poured in for the memorial fund. Mrs. Thomas smiled and swore that Chris was enjoying the whole celebration — she didn't know where, but she knew he was watching.

Dennis Kelly, meanwhile, had turned to Mr. Perillo in another part of the room. "I can't believe how many people are here."

"And every one of them has another story. I think Kevin's right: If you put them all together, you'd think they were talking about four or five different people."

"I wonder how many of the storytellers really loved him."

"When was love ever enough, Dennis? What good is it?"

"Don't say that. It was all he really wanted. He seemed to be searching for it in every contact he made. You know, until Chris died I didn't realize what he or other people meant to me. He taught me to love and care for others a little bit more."

"He was wonderful, Dennis, he really was. He made you laugh. He made it seem like anything was possible. And he made you believe in yourself. Then the day came when I thought I couldn't help him. I thought I failed him when he needed me."

"I don't think that's true. You loved him, too."

"But I never told him."

Three days later, Owen's friend Marty died suddenly, and Owen returned home for another farewell. Owen wasn't superstitious, but there were days that spring when he felt that something was pursuing him, like some kind of monster in an old children's story, or some crazed killer in a horror movie.

He was glad when he found a new job that April doing landscaping work. It was good to be outside in the sunshine working normal hours. It was quiet and peaceful tending the lawns and shrubs of the estates along the sea.

That summer when his father's restaurant reopened, they quarrelled. Owen wanted to continue the landscaping work, while his father said he needed him in the restaurant. For a few weeks Owen tried to do both jobs on alternate days, but when he was told that he had to work at the restaurant after he came home from the landscaping job, he packed his bags and headed for the train station. The trouble was that everyone found out he was leaving, and it seemed like half the town showed up at the station, too.

"C'mon, Owen, come back home."

"No, the hell with that."

"C'mon, you'll get over it."

"I'm going back to the fish market."

"Stay here, it's nice out here, much safer than the city."

"Yeah, right." Owen laughed. "Tell Chris that! I'm sure he'll be glad to hear it."

Even the landscape contractor he worked for got into the act, pleading with him to stay. Owen gave up arguing with everyone and began to look at a pretty girl named Susan who had come onto the platform. The next thing he knew he was letting the train pull out of the station without him. Susan was very petite, very pretty, and the idea of her was definitely more appealing than the Fulton Fish Market. And she thought that the handsome six-footer with the wavy blond hair looked pretty good, too.

So there Owen stayed for the next year, seeing as much of Susan as he could, working at the restaurant during the busy summer season, going back to his landscaping work in the fall, spending more of the winter back home with his mother, and returning in the spring to his work outdoors.

In the fall of 1981, however, Owen grew tired of his unsettled life. He was twenty years old now, he had already lived longer than his brother, and he had neither a diploma nor a career of any kind. He thought that if he went back to his mother's house permanently, he might start getting some credits to complete his requirements for his high school diploma and then get himself established somewhere in the fish business.

Owen went back in November to those familiar, cobblestoned streets he called "the market." It was two years now since his brother and then his friend Marty had died, and he had begun to forget about crazed killers from horror movies pursuing him. He looked at the decaying buildings and the ancient Brooklyn Bridge spanning the river to his home. He craned his neck the other way to make sure Popeye was still up there on the wall. And he was — the paint was fading, but he was still strutting and flexing that mighty bicep. Owen felt good. He smiled and said to himself, "It's not so bad here. Not exactly Lazy Pond Lane, but if my great-grandfather could make it down here I guess I can, too."

Owen took a job with the P & G Fish Company as a journeyman, which was definitely a step up from two years before. Then he had done nothing but lift and push crates of iced fish that weighed over a hundred pounds. Now he took the orders from the storeowners and assigned the new kids to load and unload the crates.

THIRTEEN

On Wednesday, December 16, Owen left work on South Street at about one P.M. He had worked longer than usual, since the predawn hours, because the company was short of help that day. Tired and hungry, he pulled on a jacket against the chill wind coming off the river and turned the corner onto Beekman Street with one of his coworkers, Jeff Martin. Jeff had a reputation for getting into trouble, but they had worked together all night and Owen felt a little sorry for him somehow, even though Jeff, at twenty-six, was almost seven years his senior. They headed away from the river to Keno's where a birthday party was being held for Jerry, another friend. After a while they left the party and turned up Beekman Street to Carmine's, an old bar like the kind Owen's grandfather went to when he worked in the fish markets.

After sausage-and-pepper heros and a mug or two of Budweiser, Owen reached for his jacket.

"Let's go, Jeff. I'm going home."

"Are you kidding? We just got here."

"No, I'm not kidding. My mother's gonna kill me as it is for taking her car without leaving a note or anything."

Owen was genuinely sorry he had done that. Despite his occasional tough-guy talk, he had always been close to his youthful mother who many took to be his sister. But for the last two years, since Chris was killed, he had become fiercely protective of her as well. After all, with his father far away and his older brother dead, someone had to be the man of the house.

"C'mon, Owen, stay for one more beer."

Owen stared right at him. "You've had enough already. You had enough at Keno's. Let's go."

"All right, all right," said Jeff grudgingly. "No sermons, just give me a ride home."

They walked out the door to Beekman Street and turned left past an open manhole in the street, where two telephone men were working on some underground cables. Owen stopped at an aging green Dodge. While fumbling distractedly for the right key, he didn't notice a young black couple walking up from South Street. But Jeff did, and by the time Owen got behind the wheel, Jeff had made a wise remark. As Owen reached over to open the other door, the couple stopped a few yards past the car and then continued walking. Owen yelled out the opened passenger door, "Get in the car!"

"No way. I'm gonna get that nigger," muttered Jeff, turning away and running after them. "Get back here, you black . . ."

Owen jumped out of the car just as Jeff lunged at his intended victim from behind.

"Get back here," yelled Owen angrily, but it was too late. As they rolled over in the gutter, Owen heard Jeff's cry. "Owen! Owen, help me!"

As he charged up the street, the black woman shouted, "Watch out, here comes the other one!" Owen caught the man in a headlock from behind, but in that thumping rush of adrenaline he didn't see the quick hand coming up underneath, glittering with sharpened silver. He didn't see Jeff wriggling away holding his bleeding arm, either. He just felt the powerful lurch of his unsought foe breaking free. While the knife plunged and ripped into him again and again, the woman screamed hysterically. To the December sky, darkening across the ancient cobblestones running with Owen's blood, it was a scream as futile as a mother's for her dead son.

Dom De Marco, working underground on the phone company lines, heard the shouting and cursing and then that piercing scream. As he came up out of his manhole he saw Owen stagger and fall to the ground. "Mom, Mom," Owen cried. "My stomach, Mom."

De Marco yelled down the manhole for his coworker to follow and then ran to Owen. He put his jacket over the dark red stain spreading fast across Owen's stomach and ran into Carmine's to get someone to call an ambulance. When he got back to Owen, the other phone company worker was hunched over at him. "He's getting real cold, Dom. I don't think he's breathing anymore."

Just then one of the phone company's white Hornets turned the corner. De Marco recognized his boss's car and flagged him down. "George, this guy's bleeding to death. We better get him over to Beekman Hospital right away. If we wait for an ambulance he'll die. The other one's okay. Just a cut arm. Put him in the backseat. Hurry."

They lifted Owen carefully. His intestines were pushing out of his stomach wound, and his shirt was a deepening red across his chest. He moaned and made a choking sound as they placed him in the front seat. Before Owen made that sound they thought he might have already died.

George slammed his hand down on the car horn and pushed his way through the traffic and red lights. Two pedestrians jumped out of his path as he screeched into the hospital driveway. He blasted the horn until a nurse came running out.

When she pulled the passenger door open, Owen began to fall out, and as she held him up she felt a mound on his stomach. It wasn't a makeshift bandage, as she first thought — it was Owen's guts.

Some attendants came running out and helped place Owen on a stretcher. A paramedic put a respirator bag over his nose and mouth to force air into his collapsed lungs. As they rushed him into the emergency room, pushing people aside, another nurse began injecting blood intravenously. Seconds later Owen was hooked up to a respirator, a machine that forces a person to breathe.

After the attendants carried Owen inside, the telephone workers who brought him there saw how big a pool of blood covered the front seat. Aside from the gasping moan when they placed him in the car, Owen had shown no sign of life on the way over. They walked inside and waited near the emergency room doors.

Meanwhile, the two young surgeons on coffee break heard their beepers signal a major trauma crisis. They raced down to the emergency room. One of them, Dr. Velez, placed his stethoscope near Owen's torn chest and heard only the faintest of sounds coming from his heart. Owen's blood pressure kept dropping, lower and lower. The doctor listened again, pressing the earplug of his stethoscope with his left hand, but he heard nothing.

One of the attendants signaled thumbs down to the two telephone men who had tried to save Owen's life. A report went out on the police radio about a homicide on Beekman Street near the markets. Owen Thomas was dead.

Dr. Velez looked up from the bloody corpse and a second passed — that's all it took for a will fiercer than medicine to say no to death. He flung his stethoscope aside and grabbed a scalpel, cutting clear across Owen's chest through an artery that had no blood left in it to spurt.

With his bare hands, the doctor spread the flesh and ribs back, pushed the useless lung aside, cut through the sac, and reached for Owen's heart. With his left hand under it, he pressed the heart with his right hand, paused, squeezed again, and paused, and then began again with infinite patience. No matter what that clock on the wall said, time was standing still. The doctor's small hands were forcing blood to Owen's brain. Machines would now have to wait for those hands, those bare human hands, to perform their simple miracle. Like a seasoned player shooting from the foul line in a tie game, he worked with icy confidence.

Dr. Velez noticed a hole in the right side of the heart that had to be sutured. While another doctor held Owen's heart, he quickly stitched the wound with silken thread. He resumed squeezing the heart to make it pump blood to the brain. Then they moved the machines and the chemicals in to keep it going: electrolyte fluids to counter the acids that were building up; lidocaine, an electrical stabilizer; electric shocks to stop spasms.

Owen's heart began to beat by itself, his blood pressure climbed, and four minutes later his lungs began to work again by themselves. He had been in the hospital for an hour now, ten minutes of which he was clinically dead, and there were at least three more hours of work to do: sewing the severed blood vessels together, repairing his slashed liver, removing his gall bladder, repairing the torn lung.

Owen's mother had a visitor late that day in her own hospital emergency room. She recognized a friend of Owen's. Again, like two years earlier, she thought he needed help for some injury. Again the shock. She called out to the first-born son she had lost two years before, "Chris, Chris, don't let this happen!" And she rushed to Owen's side.

She waited through the night, praying to her first son to save her second, trying to believe in medicine, but knowing in her nurse's heart its shortcomings. When so much damage was done to a human being, how could he live? She knew any one of his injuries was enough to kill him even though he was young and strong. And if he lived, in what condition would he live?

About five hours later, in the predawn hours of Thursday, Owen went into convulsions — a very ominous sign that his brain had been damaged by the lack of oxygen. One drug after another failed to calm his tormented body. Finally they resorted to one that in effect paralyzed him. And the long wait began. Twelve hours had now passed since the stabbing; if Owen didn't regain consciousness by the afternoon he might never. The doctors came at dawn, shining a light into Owen's eyes. The pupils were fixed and dilated — like a dead man's.

FOURTEEN

Several hours later Owen's mother stood by his bedside, bravely fighting back tears at the sight of her helpless child kept alive only by tubes and machines. No one knew better than she that he was locked in the last struggle — for breath itself. If strength and courage were all, she knew that Owen had enough to win. But Chris had been strong and brave, too.

She watched a nurse come in and check Owen's pupils for signs of brain activity, and she knew by the way the nurse rushed past her out of the room without looking into her eyes that she had found none.

Mrs. Thomas moved close to her son again and clutched his unresponding hand. "Owen," she called out softly but desperately, "you were lonely, and you wanted to see your brother." And then she cried out, "Chris, oh, Chris, I need you!" It was the everlasting cry of Mother against Death, crying out still to the smiling son torn away from her behind her back, without even the mercy of being able to fight for his life. *But not this time*, she thought as she held Owen's hands tighter, *not this time.*

At that moment one of the doctors came hurriedly into the room to Owen's bedside. He checked the pupils of his eyes again. "Owen!" he called out, "Owen!" and then pinched him as hard as he could. Mrs. Thomas never let go of her son's hand; she never took her eyes off his. And then it happened, what her undying love told her would happen — Owen blinked his eyes and moaned. He had survived, the "dead man" had survived.

After several days of slipping in and out of consciousness, Owen uttered his first words. "Oh, Mom, I'm so sorry."

"I know, Owen, I know. We were so worried about you."

"I saw Chris."

"What did you say, honey?"

"He came to me, Mom, or I came to him, I don't know. I was in a dark place. . . . I think I was standing up. . . . His voice came out to me just like it was yesterday."

"Owen, you saw Chris?"

"His hands . . . they were so big, so tremendous . . . so warm coming out to me, to my shoulders . . . his hands were so huge, but I wasn't scared."

"Did Chris speak? Did he say something?"

"He said, 'No, you can't come here. There's no room for you here!' And those big hands just pushed me back down. It was as real as talking to you right now."

Just when did this astounding visit take place? Was it at the moment Dr. Velez threw his stethoscope aside, cut Owen's chest open, and took his heart into his bare hands, making it beat when it had given up? Was it at the moment Owen's gentle mother said to Death, "No, you have taken one from my eyes. You shall not have another"?

And just how does such a miracle happen? Is it so hard to believe that someone died and lived again? Is it any more incomprehensible than the miracle of being born — it's a hundred million to one — in the first place?

Christopher and Owen Thomas had been separated by many small things in their lifetimes, and by an eternity in their deaths. But if Chris could show Kevin and Dennis and Dee and Joe the way to believe and to love, if he could remain for Dan Perillo a bright flame in a dark and mindless sea, why could he not do this small favor for his own brother?

The golden friend who never would grow old had not squandered his smile beyond recall; he had kept it alive for those few who knew all, yet kept their love undiminished and untarnished. The luster of a great basketball victory would in time be dimmed, but not a brother's love. This would remain — stronger than death, a dream beyond glory.